RAISING
EMPOWERED
ATHLETES

RAISING EMPOWERED ATHLETES

A Youth Sports Parenting Guide for Raising
Happy, Brave, and Resilient Kids

Kirsten Jones

TRIUMPH
BOOKS

This book is available in quantity at special discounts for your group or organization. For further information, contact:

Triumph Books LLC
814 North Franklin Street
Chicago, Illinois 60610
(312) 337-0747
www.triumphbooks.com

Printed in U.S.A.
ISBN: 978-1-63727-281-7
Design by Nord Compo

To Brian Reynolds
(January 28, 1972–August 7, 2022),
a dear friend and youth sports coach who
focused on what mattered most: the kids.

It is not the critic who counts; not the man who points out how the strong man stumbles, or where the doer of deeds could have done them better. The credit belongs to the man who is actually in the arena, whose face is marred by dust and sweat and blood; who strives valiantly; who errs, who comes short again and again, because there is no effort without error and shortcoming; but who does actually strive to do the deeds; who knows great enthusiasms, the great devotions; who spends himself in a worthy cause; who at the best knows in the end the triumph of high achievement, and who at the worst, if he fails, at least fails while daring greatly, so that his place shall never be with those cold and timid souls who neither know victory nor defeat.

—Theodore Roosevelt, 26th
president of the United States

CONTENTS

**Part IV: Strategy III:
Appreciating Team & Coach Dynamics**

Part V: Strategy IV: Dreaming Big

AUTHOR'S NOTE

Just before a game begins, it's common for coaches to send their teams onto the field or court with a few final bits of instructions. Before you begin my book, here are mine:

First, it's not about a particular sport. Period. It's about your son or daughter—and how you can raise him or her to be an empowered human being. I use examples from numerous sports but made no attempt to be equal in my references to each. I would encourage you to focus not on the context of the sport but on the message within sport.

Second, it's not about the gender of your son or daughter. In some cases, I refer to female athletes, at times to males. With some obvious exceptions, much of what I share as an author and sports-parenting coach are applicable to both.

Third, it's not about socioeconomics. I live and work in Southern California, where there's an abundance of well-to-do families who can afford private coaching, club teams, and $200 basketball shoes. But if that's the context I know, I also know that my insight is equal-opportunity stuff, applicable to families regardless of where they live or their yearly income.

Fourth, I have attempted to write a book that, as a parent raising three kids, I'd want to read. It is not an academic treatise. It is, I hope, parent-friendly, written from someone who was a former Division I athlete, who coaches athletes on and off the court as well as parents, but who, above all, is a parent of athletes herself.

Finally, it's not about raising a professional athlete or even a Division I athlete. This is about raising kids who, regardless of how high they climb on the athletic ladder, might become kind, compassionate, confident, well-focused young adults who passionately pursue their goals. Sometimes they will succeed, sometimes they will fail, but my hope is that we raise young people gritty enough that when they do fall down, they dust themselves off and begin anew.

Now, who's with me? Let's do this!

Part 1

HOW AND WHEN DID YOUTH SPORTS GET SO CRAZY?

CHAPTER ONE

WHATEVER HAPPENED TO REC BALL?

Youth sports aren't what they used to be

Meet one of my son's former teammates, Jake. He's the 14-year-old kid over there who walks as if he's 85, bent over like a question mark. That's his father, Tom, the one whose eyes get all glassy-eyed when I ask him why he thinks it happened—why a teenager with all the potential in the world wound up with a pars stress fracture in his back.

"Bad parenting," Tom says. "We never should have signed him up for two club sports—soccer and basketball—that, beyond game time, involved far too many hours training."

That's a harsh self-evaluation—and honorable, I think, in its honesty. But in my eight years as a sports-parenting coach, I've dealt with hundreds of young people and their families, and when things go wrong, it's usually not because of bad parenting. It's because of lost-perspective parenting. Snow-plow parenting. Drone parenting. FOMO (fear of missing out) parenting.

Unrealistic parenting. Parenting as if you suddenly found your-self in a youth sports jungle that resembles nothing of the "rec ball" days you remembered from your youth—and you fell into a few snake pits because of it.

Hey, we're not all Indiana Jones. Besides being a Peak Per-formance coach, I'm also a mom of three young athletes, one of whom, Caelan (who goes by CJ), reached a lifelong goal and is now a Division I basketball player, and another one, Parker, who soon will be. Anyone who's heard my podcasts or heard me speak to parents knows that when it comes to hacking our way through the ever-changing youth sports jungle, I've fallen into a few sports-parenting traps myself. Like when my daughter, Kylie, made a highly competitive volleyball team but (rightfully) didn't get to play for an entire season (but it still sucked). Man, it is so hard to sit on the sidelines and watch your kid not get subbed in the entire season! Or the time CJ lost in the state high school boys' basketball quarterfinals to a team they had beaten. As a parent, listening to your child quietly weep from the backseat in the car ride home just guts you. You know there is nothing you can do to fix their pain. Or when my middle son, Parker, was convinced he was the worst player on the court and didn't think he'd ever been good enough to play in college. Helping your child build belief in themselves can be so challenging when they don't believe anything Mom, Dad, or Coach says.

I could go on. There are too many moments to count. But in short, we're in this together, baby; I'm here to help!

Most parents want what's best for their children; we just get caught up in the king-of-the-mountain game. And then bad things happen to good families.

Take Jake, my lead-off story. He was a talented soccer player from an early age. With size, speed, natural athleticism, and an off-the-charts athletic IQ, he was like the Wayne Gretzky of youth soccer; he didn't run to where the ball was, he ran to where it *was going to be*. Tom, his father, grew up playing and loving soccer in his native South Africa; all he wanted was for his son to share his passion for the game.

In 2016, at the age of 13, Jake was moving on from AYSO (rec soccer) to join a highly touted soccer club in Southern California. But in addition to playing club soccer, Jake loved basketball and played on a middle school and a club team. His parents knew little about basketball but could see that their son had passion for the sport. They also realized that because he hit puberty early, he had the size and physicality to be great; he dominated the prepubescent late-bloomers in hoops, too.

How could they *not* encourage such talent? So they did. Weekends became a blur, the family driving from this practice to that game, from this sport to that sport. Jake's schedule often looked like this:

Friday 5 PM to 7 PM: Soccer practice
Saturday 8 AM: Basketball practice
10 AM: Soccer game
1 PM: Soccer game
4 PM: Soccer game
Sunday 9 AM: Basketball game
11 AM: Soccer game
1 PM: Basketball game

And this was just on the weekend. During the week, multiple practices and conditioning sessions sucked time from the family. School, practice, games, rinse, repeat. "Free time?" What was that?

Despite the frenetic schedule, Tom was thrilled that Jake was having fun and getting lots of playing time—he always started and was hardly subbed out—so both parents supported the challenge of Jake juggling both sports while managing to keep his grades up without breaking a sweat.

Then, seemingly without advanced warning, the payment came due. In a summer basketball game prior to his freshman year of high school, Jake went up for a rebound and his back seized up so badly the pain dropped him to his knees. He couldn't walk. He was later diagnosed with a pars stress fracture in his back. Stress fractures are caused by "monotonous and repetitive loading of the back," a code phrase for "overuse." Youth are particularly prone to this because their bone structure isn't fully developed yet. When you combine hours of play each day for six or seven days a week, little rest, and hard-working growth plates, you end up with chronic injury.

Youth sports participation has dramatically increased over the last two decades, according to the National Youth Sports Health and Safety Institute. Approximately 45 million children aged 6–18 participate in some form of organized athletics. If that's not particularly alarming, this is: roughly half of all injuries evaluated in pediatric sports medicine clinics are associated with one thing.

Overuse. Kids like Jake and fathers like Tom who didn't know when to say "when."

"Jake loved every minute of it," Tom told me. "But right now he's absolutely miserable and we feel incredibly guilty for not making better choices for his health because he wasn't old enough to understand the potential risks."

He paused. "I'd like a do-over. I know I wouldn't make those same those same mistakes again."

How Yesterday Changed Today

Question one: How did we get here—to this place where youth sports, which are inherently supposed to be fun and teach us an array of life lessons, have become a source of relentless pressure, heartache, and disappointment?

To the place where our children's backs crumble because of overuse—and the bond that drew a father and son together shatters like glass?

To the place where the average 15-year-old competitive athlete will be involved in eight to 10 workouts a week?

To the place where 70 percent of children are dropping out of sports by age 13?

To the place where youth sports is now a $20-plus billion industry, exceeding the amount of money generated by the NFL. One in five U.S. families spends more than $12,000 a year on youth sports.

This is not the youth sports we Generation Xers all fondly recall from our childhoods, where we all played at least two or three different sports, our parents were barely involved, and very few of us gave a second thought about playing past high school.

Question two: How do we get *out* of this jungle—to the place where sports are fun, and kids look forward to participating instead of dreading it?

To the place where sports help our children become healthier adults who are more likely to be active, suffer less anxiety, and are better suited to handle stress throughout life?

To the place where everything isn't about selling one's soul to the devil of win-win-win and everyone gets a trophy?

To the place where there's some sort of practical compromise between "DI or bust" and "just roll out the ball and let them kick it around."

If you're asking yourself those two questions (*How did we get here?* and *How do we get out of here?*), you've come to the right place for answers. That's what this book is all about. About finding that sweet spot between sports as part of a young person's life and sports *as* his or her life. About raising kids who are not only passionate about life on the court or field but curious about life beyond the out-of-bounds lines. About teaching your kids that it's a competitive world—without being the disgruntled parent who, to shame a baseball coach for not playing his kid, hires a skywriter to buzz the stadium with a "Coach Sucks" banner. (Yes, as you'll read later, that actually *did* happen.)

How did we get to this point? How did we lose perspective? Because we Generation X (Gen X) parents have become the proverbial frog in the pot, slowly boiling to death because of benign neglect—instead of heeding the warnings from raised-to-be-a-star types like Andre Agassi, Tiger Woods, and Todd Marinovich. Back in the 1980s, we Gen Xers were so mesmerized by their successes that years later, when we became parents, we failed to realize the price those athletes paid for that success.

We didn't learn from the past. Instead, parents started to ask what it would take to get their child to an elite level. And how did these child prodigies manage do it at such a young age? They wondered what would happen if more focused time and attention were placed on nurturing their child's sports "career"—as if they were business associates, not kids. While parents of previous generations didn't give their kids' athletic futures a second thought, this new generation of parents saw a possibility rarely witnessed: creating future stars. College scholarships. Prestigious universities. Fame. Fortune. The possibilities danced in the minds of parents who wondered, *Can I too, raise a Serena Williams?*

And because we didn't learn from the past, that's why we'd be foolish to not try to understand it. Let's take a moment to look back. Generally, here's how it unfolded:

Growing up in the 1970s and '80s, the rage of fashion was painter pants, puffy vests, Nike Cortez running shoes, and heavily permed haircuts with enough Aqua Net to hold your feathered Shaun Cassidy shag "do" in place. In 1981, Music Television (MTV) appeared on the big boxes in our living rooms for the first time, forever changing the way we viewed, listened to, and appreciated music. We sat glued to the screens seeing our favorite artists, including Foreigner, The Rolling Stones, Cyndi Lauper, The Police, and Bon Jovi. "I Want My MTV," performed by Dire Straits, was belted out by teens across America.

Simultaneously, a parental shift was rippling across the country, even if few noticed at the time—and some never noticed it, period. Three major sociological developments led to significant changes in the way people parented. The trifecta of youth-sports craziness triggered a decline in recreation (rec) youth sports over the next 20 years, the vacuum of which was filled by the professionalization of kids' leagues that looked nothing like their predecessor.

Three Factors That Changed Youth Sports

First, family life changed dramatically. By the early 1970s, women began joining the workforce and by the 1980s, two-income families were common. Among married women ages 25 to 44, 26 percent worked outside of the home in the 1950s. By the mid-1980s, this number had grown to 67 percent. Dads were gone all day. Moms were gone all day. And so a new problem arose: What were the kids supposed to do after school and on weekends so that they wouldn't be left unattended? (Hint: sports!)

Second, children in the United States began falling behind on the global academic front. The 1983 National Commission on Excellence in Education report, famously titled "A Nation at Risk," touched off a wave of local, state, and federal reform efforts. Parents started to panic that their children were falling behind academically. How would parents solve this gap? (Hint: getting more involved in their children's academics!) This would lead to a parental shift that involved Mom and Dad spending more time doing homework with (for?) their kids, hiring tutors, and starting to micromanage their children's academic lives.

Their obsession with that naturally carried over to their children's sports worlds, too.

Third, in 1981, six-year-old Adam John Walsh was abducted and murdered in Hollywood, Florida. His severed head was found in a drainage canal. His death attracted national attention and led to the 1983 television film *Adam*, seen by 38 million people in its original airing. Parents began worrying that their children would no longer be safe playing in their neighborhoods unsupervised until dark; the days of letting kids basically create their own fun were over, replaced by adult-led programs, teams, leagues, organizations, and clubs—the operative phrase being "adult-led."

"Create your own fun" was out. Structure was in. "Be on your own" was out. Parental involvement was in.

Never mind that the Adam Walsh murder led to widely exaggerated missing-children statistics and unfounded fears. Perception, as they say, is everything, and even if the problem wasn't that serious, "stranger danger" increased the sense of urgency and inflamed the dread of parents, children, and others concerned with child safety.

These three cultural shifts—mothers joining the workforce, parents doubling down to make their kids academic wizards, and the fear of child abduction—made the landscape ripe for a sea change involving children, period. And on September 7, 1979, something debuted that would give that sea change a sports twist: Entertainment and Sports Programming Network launched. Like a flat-screened Pied Piper, ESPN burst on the scene with round-the-clock sports, there to fill the vacuum for kids who, in earlier times, would have simply "gone outside and played."

Suddenly, athletes were front and center on televisions across America. Youth sports prodigies who may have gone unnoticed in previous years were running, throwing, tackling, flipping, shooting, swinging, and spiking their ways into the imaginations of kids from Malibu to Maine. Hockey's Gretzky, tennis' Andre Agassi, golf's Tiger Woods, and gymnastics' Nadia Comaneci—such young superstars were, seemingly overnight, part of our children's lives. And part of our lives as parents.

Light bulbs began turning on in the minds of parents all over the country: "Our kid could be the next Gretzky, Agassi, Woods, Comaneci!"—pick your prodigy. Subconsciously, parents began thinking, *What better way to keep my child safe, supervised, and focused?* They also began realizing that this wasn't going to happen without a major commitment of time, effort, money, and "aggressive involvement," much of which, of course, would prove counterproductive.

They didn't have to look far for inspiration. In the early 1970s, former Iranian boxer-turned-Las-Vegas-tennis-pro Emmanuel (Mike) Agassi decided his fourth child would become a world-class tennis player. Unaware of any formula to mastery but determined to see one of his children succeed where he had failed as an Olympic boxer (1948 and 1952), Mike put a plan in place to create a tennis prodigy.

Legend has it that he actually taped a ping pong paddle to Andre's hand while he lay in the crib. In 1977, when Andre was seven years old, the ball machine—nicknamed "The Dragon" by his dad—had become "abject horror" to the young boy.

"Nothing sends my father into a rage like hitting a ball into the net," he wrote in his bestseller *Open: An Autobiography*. "He foams at the mouth.... My arm feels like it's going to fall off. I want to ask: How much longer, Pops? But I don't ask. I hit as hard as I can, then slightly harder.... My father says that if I hit 2,500 balls each day, I'll hit 17,500 balls each week, and at the end of one year I'll have hit nearly one million balls. He believes in math. Numbers, he says, don't lie. A child who hits one million balls each year will be unbeatable."

Andre remembers standing on the tennis court in their family's backyard, a court his father built by hand himself. He didn't have an inch to move, the entire court covered in fuzzy yellow balls. He had spent the previous three hours in the 100-plus-degree Vegas summer heat trying to beat The Dragon.

At 13, he was shipped off to Nick Bollettieri's Tennis Academy in Bradenton, Florida, though he didn't want to leave Las Vegas or his friends or family. But ultimately the commitment paid off. Agassi became an eight-time Grand Slam champion, won an Olympic gold medal in 1996, and amassed total tennis earnings of close to $200 million.

K. Anders Ericsson, a Swedish psychologist at Florida State University, argued in his 1990 book *Toward a General Theory of Expertise* that anyone who puts in 10,000 hours of practice at any activity (chess, darts, or yes, sports) could become an expert. And there was no shortage of parents willing to test the theory.

"ROBO QUARTERBACK"

Take the Marinovich family of Orange County, California. Marv and his son Todd were football's equivalent of Mike and Andre Agassi. In 1988, *Sports Illustrated (SI)* dubbed Todd America's first "test-tube athlete." When Todd was one month old, Marv was already working on his son's physical conditioning. He stretched his hamstrings. Taught him to do pushups. Kept a football in his crib 24/7.

As a toddler, Todd was placed on a strict diet. When he went to birthday parties as a kid, he would take his own cake and ice cream to avoid sugar and refined white flour. He would eat homemade catsup, prepared with honey. No Big Macs. No Oreos. No deviating from Dad's plan.

Eventually, Marv brought in a team of 13 individuals to work on every aspect of Todd's physical condition—speed, agility, strength, flexibility, quickness, body control, endurance, and nutrition. He found one to improve Todd's peripheral vision. He enlisted a throwing coach, a motion coach, and a psychologist.

"I'm a tyrant," Marv told *SI.* "But I think you have to be to succeed."

His son's athletic career was mixed. As a redshirt freshman in 1989, he became the starting quarterback at University of Southern California and was chosen as the country's freshman of the year. Two years later he entered the NFL because of a fallout with Coach Larry Smith and an arrest for cocaine; he signed with the Los Angeles Raiders. But three years later he was already out of the NFL, largely because of his inability to kick drugs. Since then, he's been in and out of prison, most recently in 2018—at age 48.

If the demands put on Agassi and Marinovich by their fathers inspired some other parents to set the bar high for their sports-oriented children, they also raise questions: Is it worth it? How much is too much? How do you find balance? Can you raise athletically successful children without turning them into "projects" or "experiments?" And, finally, is it possible to inspire your athletically-oriented children to be the best they can be without becoming, as a parent, "a tyrant?"

Andre and his wife, Stephanie Graf, a tennis legend in her own right and a survivor of a parenting tyrant herself, went on to have two children of their own. Because of the grueling childhoods they'd had, they agreed not encourage their children to play tennis but rather choose whatever activity appealed to them.

A few years after Andre's retirement from tennis, his aging dad confessed to him that if he could do it all over again, he wouldn't have made him play tennis, either. "I'd make you play baseball or golf. You can play for longer and make a lot more money."

CHAPTER TWO

WHOSE DREAM IS IT?

Our child's wants and needs aren't always our own

AS THE YOUNGEST OF FOUR CHILDREN, Jennifer would rather lose a limb than lose to one of her siblings in anything from racing to the dinner table to slaying a TikTok dance-off. In order to keep up with her two sisters and brother, she developed a binary mindset that left no space for anything other than one possibility: to win.

Athletics, of course, are the perfect outlet for such determination. Soon after starting middle school in 2012, Jennifer emerged as a standout lacrosse player—and born natural leader. She was voted captain of her team and won multiple leadership awards from her peers. With an ever-present smile and happy-go-lucky personality, she made whatever she worked at look effortless.

From the get-go, her mother, Lisa, was like lacrosse's answer to Geppetto, Pinocchio's father. With great passion, she began puppeteering her daughter's destiny. Having already successfully launched three older children, two of whom had played lacrosse at the Division II (DII) college level, Lisa was certain she knew exactly what it would take to help her fourth child reach the DI pinnacle.

With the wisdom of experience—and without so much as a consult with her daughter—Lisa was certain she had a clear vision of her daughter's dream school: one ranked at the top of *US News and World Reports'* Best Colleges with not only high-caliber athletics but also top-ranked academics. Jennifer's siblings had attended high academic schools, but they didn't have strong teams. Lisa wanted "the trifecta" for Jennifer: great athletics, top academics, and a close-to-home location, preferably only a few hours from the family home in Northern Virginia. Lisa wanted to be able to attend all of her daughter's college games, something she wasn't able to do with her other children.

When Jennifer made a highly competitive lacrosse club in Northern Virginia, Lisa liked to be "in the know" about every girl on the team. Most parents let the girls' engineer the conversation on the way to and from practice from the back of the SUV; not Lisa.

"She was always asking questions about what camps or clinics I was going to as well as if I'd heard from any colleges regarding recruiting," said one of Jennifer's club teammates. "It wasn't inappropriate, but she was definitely more focused on controlling the conversation. Most parents just crank up the tunes, let us chill in the back, and leave us to our own silly banter."

Lisa finagled a volunteer position, becoming part of "mission control" for the club. She served as the club's office manager, which allowed her access to information of every family in the club. She watched over the program like a red-tailed hawk that sits high in a tree, purveying its territory. She would spot her prey, lock in, and swoop in for the informational kill. Boom. She learned which girls were getting recruited by which colleges. Boom. She learned what each player's GPA was. Boom. She learned which families went to every showcase event attended by college coaches interested in recruiting the top high school prospects.

All for the purpose of helping her best position Jennifer for that DI scholarship.

Jennifer had it all. In addition to athleticism and speed, lacrosse coaches look for size. By age 16, Jennifer's lanky frame and blond ponytail caught the eyes of many college coaches. Taking no chances, Lisa would bring x-rays to tournaments to show college coaches what doctors had apparently told her: that Jennifer's growth plates were still "wide open." Indeed, there was a good possibility that her daughter would reach six feet in height.

By now, the question begging for an answer is: Uh, what about Jennifer? We know she's an outstanding lacrosse player, but is her mother's DI dream *her* daughter's dream, too? Is Jennifer OK with a mother who's become an uninvited public relations manager?

Be a Potter, Not a Promoter

Before we continue, let's just come right out and say it: don't be the mom who flaunts your child's x-rays on the sideline. There should be some sort of warning light that comes on for youth-sports parents who go to such lengths: *Danger! Danger! Your child is a living, breathing human being! Don't try to promote her like she's a product. And don't assume you know what she wants.*

Instead of being an agent for your kid, be a potter. There is an art to making ceramic pottery. It takes more than just slapping some wet clay on a spinning wheel, adding water, and waiting for a beautiful piece of art to emerge. The process requires multiple steps, which include having the proper tools. You need a wheel, a bucket of water, the right type and amount of clay, some straightforward instructions, a vision for what you'd like to create, and a whole lot of practice with pots becoming teacups to produce something other than an ashtray that eventually becomes a coin receptacle.

Being a sports parent today is like being a potter. It's a lot like molding clay. There are some "givens," such as the amount of raw talent your child has and his or her DNA, which will dictate their eventual size and general athletic ability. But more important are several intangible factors that will determine their long-term success: intrinsic drive (Does your child want this as badly as you do?), passion for sports (Do they really love this activity?), and competitive spirit (Do they really love to win?).

These, combined with what I call a strong "growth mindset," will factor greatly into the final trajectory your child may take. We'll dive deeper into growth mindset in Chapter 11. But beyond these "fixed" factors, a growth mindset refers to an athlete's willingness—and ability—to be curious about learning new skills. Is she open to changing her perspective about a sports situation she's facing—say, how spending some bench time might actually help her in the long run? Will she accept feedback to make adjustment? Does she understand the proverbial "there's no 'I' in team" adage?

A dear friend, Kristin Keefe, was a tennis and basketball player until, at 13, she was introduced to volleyball. In her first year, her club coach, Jeff Porter, remembers, "She was tall and skinny like a giraffe. She was all elbows and was often a heap on the floor after attempting to spike the ball." But within a few short months she had grown into her 6'1" body and her skills all came together. By her senior year in high school, she was Player of the Year for the California Interscholastic Federation (CIF) in Los Angeles and was on her way to Stanford on a volleyball scholarship.

A funny thing happened when she got to Stanford, though. "You're goofy-footed," her coach said. In her approach to spike the ball, she took off as a left-handed person would, with her last two steps being left-right. Right-handed hitters usually approach the opposite way in order to get more power and mobility into their swing. She'd always done it "backward," but nobody had corrected her, and she'd managed to get along just fine. But her coach believed the change, even this "late" into her career, would benefit her.

It was like Tiger Woods' swing coach, Butch Harmon, wanting to change Tiger's swing in 1997 after he'd won three PGA events, including the Masters, in his first year on tour. *Really? This is wise? What about that "don't-fix-it-if-it-ain't-broke" axiom?* In Tiger's case, Harmon's fix helped Tiger hit the ball even farther. In the year following the adjustment, Tiger walked away with nine PGA Tour wins. But that may not have happened had he not been open to learning an entirely new cadence and swing.

Kristin was the same way. While many top athletes' egos would have calcified them with a fixed mindset, unwilling to change, the first thing Kristin did was accept her coach's advice.

"What else can I do to improve?" she asked.

That is textbook "growth mindset." She went on to become a four-time All-American, the 1991 Women's National Player of the Year, and a member of the 1996 USA Women's Olympic volleyball team in Atlanta.

What will determine how the final "artwork" turns out involving your child and sports? The mindset and skillset of both potter and art—you and your child—regarding:

- Relying on positive "self-talk"
- Seeing effort as the path to mastery
- Embracing, rather than running away from, challenges
- Finding lessons and inspiration in the successes of others, not seeing them as a threat
- Persisting in the face of setbacks

All of these are a team effort, guided by you, the potter. If the only voice in your child's head is that of a parent saying "you're lazy" or "you're too small" or "you're not as good as so-and-so," the kid will inevitably find a way to live "down" to that statement. On the other hand, if a young athlete hears a parent saying "great hustle tonight" or "the harder you work, the better you get" or "you 'broke' No. 15's ankles on that sweet crossover you made to the basket," the child will live "up" to the statement. Remember: the voice that resonates most deeply in their head will be your voice—for better or worse.

When we fight for limitations, unfortunately we get to keep them.

Why not make it positive?

Lost Perspective

Michael was an average-sized middle school athlete from Amherst, New York, who played football, basketball, and baseball. His dad, Matt, was a lanky 6'6" and had played basketball at a local DII college. He wanted his son to become a good athlete as well, but his comments at every post-game BBQ played as if on repeat: "When I was Michael's age, I was working hard on my own. No one ever helped me. Back in my day, if you wanted it, you'd be out there, rain or shine."

But when asked if he'd ever go out and shoot around with his son he'd say, "Nah! He's too lazy to practice. He'd rather be inside playing the 'dumb box' [aka Matt's pejorative reference to the Xbox] than working on his game. He's never going to be any good because he doesn't want to work on his own. I never had help and I played in college. Why should he need it?"

In situations like this, you can assume that much of that negative talk was, at times, aimed directly at the son himself. In fact, it's probably why Michael quit playing basketball in seventh grade. A late bloomer, he grew like a sequoia in his mid-teens and by the time he was a junior in high school, he was 6'6". The varsity basketball coach took notice. He talked Michael into trying out and he played the sport he loved as a young boy for two years. But the three critical years he missed couldn't be made up.

"It's too bad he stopped playing for those three years," his coach said after he'd graduated. "He could have been really a very strong player, but with the lack of consistency in developing the fundamentals, he fell too far behind the others."

So, Jennifer, the lacrosse player, and Michael, the basketball player, were influenced by two very different types of parents. Jennifer's mother believed so strongly in her daughter's abilities that she allowed that belief to skew her sensibilities as a mother and made getting a DI scholarship more important than her daughter's desires and wishes. Michael's father, on the other hand, believed so little in his son's abilities that he allowed his own negativism to torpedo what might have been a promising high school basketball career for his son, maybe more.

They had one thing in common: both parents had lost perspective.

Reaching for the Golden Ticket

It's understandable why parents sometimes lose their way in supporting their young athletes. Most never played sports beyond high school. Sports, in their era, were low key and not ultra-competitive. All of these factors combined with societal FOMO—fear of missing out—dictate when, how, how much, and why we make the parenting choices we do.

Parents invest thousands of dollars a year and hundreds of hours into club sports. So it's understandable that we can get caught up in obsessing about a "golden ticket," the college scholarship. It stands to reason that if the neighbor boy has figured it out, why not us? When you learn that NCAA Division I and II schools provide more than $2.9 billion in athletics scholarships annually to more than 150,000 student-athletes—Division III and Ivy League (which are DI) schools don't offer athletic scholarships—the sheer numbers shout optimism: *Wow, my kid certainly can cash in on at least some of that dough!*

But assuming your eight-year-old is going to wind up being even a DI athlete, much less a professional athlete, is like assuming that buying a lottery ticket will mean you're going to be rich in ten years. It's possible, yes. But rarer than many parents realize. The competition is staggering.

Here's the reality: fewer than 8 percent of high school athletes (about 1 in 14) go on to play a varsity sport at any collegiate level and fewer than 2 percent of high school athletes (1 in 54) are awarded athletic scholarships to compete in college, according to the NCAA. (The new transfer portal has made it even more difficult because college athletes used to have to sit out a year to move to another school, leaving more spots open for incoming freshmen, which is no longer the case. More on this in Chapter 17.)

If I told you there was a 2 percent chance of rain in today's forecast, would you take an umbrella with you? No. But that's the kind of unrealistic expectations we're foisting on our kids today. We're putting the pressure of being part of that 2 percent. Many parents are not only expecting to beat the odds but naively planning on it. And, frankly, that blind optimism often contributes to an athletic experience for your child that's long on pressure and short on satisfaction.

You may, at this point, say, "Well, not me. I don't care if my kid plays sports in college, I just would like them to be active through high school," which used to seem like a reasonable expectation. But even that goal in some larger, more competitive high schools is a steep hill to climb. With the increasing 24/7 evolution of year-round sports, if your child hasn't played a sport competitively starting in grade school, odds are stacked against them making the high school team.

And while it's becoming more competitive to make the high school team there is, by contrast, an overall decline in youth sports participation in the last few decades. Did you notice that concerning statistic I've already mentioned? Seven in ten kids drop out of sports by age 13. Why? Because they aren't having fun anymore. Why? Largely because the adults—parents and coaches—are sucking the fun out of it.

With so much pressure to succeed, what kid wants to go out into the driveway and shoot until it gets dark like we did when we were growing up? Kids are saying, "Screw that! I'll go hang out with friends, play a video game, or scroll mindlessly through social media. Who needs the stress?" Some, unfortunately, make even worse choices, often involving drugs, crime, and other you-get-the-idea routes.

The effect of kids dropping out of sports at such an early age is dire. Lack of physical activity can lead to increased rates of anxiety, depression, and obesity. A year-long study by the Canadian Health Board found that young adults still active by age 24 had a high chance of continuing to be active the remainder of their lives, which leads to a happier, healthier, and more well-adjusted adulthood. This kind of benefit has nothing to do with playing at the highest levels. It's about playing, period. But why play, too many kids are asking, if it's not fun?

The problem is that too many parents think they have only two choices when it comes to youth sports: all-in or all-out. Swept up by the changing times and fearful at the sound of the herd thundering forward with the DI-or-bust attitude, they push their kids relentlessly as if the only goal is winning the lottery. Or they bag it, brand youth sports as an evil they want no part of—and rob their kid of a chance to learn and grow.

It Doesn't Have to Be Either/Or

But, folks, I'm here to tell you: there is a middle ground. I know that as a sports and life coach. I know that as a youth sports podcaster. And I know that as a parent of young athletes.

That said, I won't kid around: you might need to buck the system, the herd, the craziness to make it happen.

James Lowe, aka Coach Ballgame, is a baseball coach for kids ages 4–12 in Orange County, California. His camps and clinics focus on fun and fundamentals. The program offers "sandlot games" where all kids get to play and, amid the learning, there's a premium placed on enjoyment. He said he first realized how important his camps were when a dad of a five-year-old came up to him at the start of one.

"We're giving baseball one *last* try," he said.

"I'm sorry," said Coach Ballgame. "You said your son is five. *One last try?*"

"Yes, he's already tried two other leagues which have left him in tears and hating the game. I played baseball growing up and loved it. It's crushing me that I had to drag him here today like it's going to be torture."

Something is seriously wrong with youth sports when a five-year-old is ready to hang up the cleats because he isn't having any fun. But this isn't some sort of isolated incident.

A six-year-old in West Los Angeles, for the second year in a row, failed to make the rec baseball team. "Sorry," the confused mother was told, "we don't feel like it's fair to put Jimmy on a team now, only for him to get cut next year. Our coaching staff is already looking at how they want this team to develop in the next several years and we just don't think he has what it takes. Try the league in Santa Monica; it's a lot less competitive."

There's the 13-year-old at a West Los Angeles club soccer game, where the star player got a red card in the semifinal match for a rule violation. (Getting a red card means the player has to sit out the next game.) Not wanting to lose his star player in the finals, the coach wrote down another child's number, ensuring that the player who *shouldn't* have been able to play *would* play, but that the one who *should have* been able to play *would not*. Parents from both sides sat in stunned silence during the finals knowing full well the boy shouldn't play, and parents and coaches allowed it.

In Oregon, an umpire called a youth baseball game after four innings because of the "mercy rule." When the losing coach talked the winning coach into playing a few more innings, without umpires, the lead-off batter for the team that had just won 20–0 stepped into the box to lead off the inning. "Hey, Coach," he said to his manager at third base, "are we just playing for fun now?"

How have we come to a place where children think the default format for sports is *not* fun? I wish every youth sports mom and dad would stick a Post-It on their mirror during the season that said: GOAL NO. 1: FUN!

If you're that parent in the mirror, help foster a sense of fun and passion in your kids when it comes to sports. Kids should be enjoying the experience whether they're an outstanding athlete or not. Who knows what the future holds? Make it fun. *Now.* That will benefit not only you and your child but the coach and team. Because the only way youth sports are going to change is if enough parents recalibrate their priorities, renew their perspectives, and revitalize their own family's approach to the games. No "winning-is-the-only-thing" coach can lead if there's nobody behind him, following. That doesn't mean starting a revolution; it simply means refocusing your perspective.

To give yourself perspective as a parent, ask yourself two hard questions about you, your child, and the kid's participation—and interest—in sports:

- First, is your primary goal to have your child stay active, learn new skills, and make friends, or is your goal to see them play at the highest level possible? Both can be correct answers, but it's important to be honest with *why* you want them playing sports.
- Second, are you overly passionate about living through your child and dreaming of reaping all the glory and accolades that comes with it? Or do you not give much thought to what level team they are on or whether they get much playing time? It's understandable and acceptable to be passionate about their sports. What's important is understanding how you're responding to your child's participation and whether your involvement is helping or hurting their growth and whatever goal is in place.

Whatever the reason your child is playing sports, the better you understand the "why" behind it, the easier it will be to separate yourself from their journey. Because ultimately, it is your child's journey, not yours.

Lisa, the x-ray-toting lacrosse mom, believed she needed to control her daughter Jennifer's athletic destiny rather than encourage her from the sidelines. Instead of embedding herself into her daughter's lacrosse program, Lisa would have done better to ask her daughter what *she* wanted. Among the questions that needed answering:

- What were Jennifer's priorities for college? Did they mirror her parents' priorities?
- How important is it for Jennifer to go to a high-academic institution? What is she interested in studying—or, down the road, might be interested in doing for a career? If she is unclear about what she might be interested in majoring, which schools offer programs that hold general interest for

her? If she's a Science, Technology, Engineering, and Math (STEM)-focused kid, the list of schools will be completely different than if she's more of a creative writing and art kid.

- If Jennifer wants to play lacrosse in college, what level does she desire to play? DI, DII, or DIII? Why does she want to play? Can she articulate her passion? Is it about being on a team or is it the sport itself? Getting clear on her "why" is important in finding the right fit of athletic program and school.

- If Jennifer gets interest from schools, what are the driving factors that will help make the final decision for her? Location? What majors the school offers? Level of play? Greek life?

Nothing crushes a college coach's spirit more than to hear that the parent is making the decision for the child. Yes, the parent should be there to guide her, but not allowing her to have major input into the largest decision of her life, thus far, will almost certainly backfire.

Former NFL cornerback Derek Cox, a past client of mine, was fortunate to have parents with perspective. "My parents' advice was, 'This is your life. It's your choice.' And that was very empowering later when I was in college and things weren't necessarily going that well. I called home to complain about the tough practices and the difficult classes and my mom didn't miss a beat. She simply reiterated what they had said earlier. She was right. This was my choice. I needed to own it and work through it."

Despite playing at a smaller DIAA school, the College of William & Mary, Cox got drafted by an NFL team and spent seven years in the league. He recalls college teammates who didn't have a say in where they were going to college. Their parents decided for them. "When times got tough, they bailed because they had no ownership of the decision." They didn't see it as their responsibility to learn from it and so they didn't learn, they just passed the buck.

For Jennifer, all the questions listed above needed to be taken into account in order for her to make the most educated decision she could and be motivated to work through both the highs and the lows. Because there are no guarantees in life. If you really want to achieve something meaningful, you need to be willing to work hard even when it's not fun or easy.

In her case, Jennifer ended up going to the high-academic school, even though she frequently told her carpool friends that the choice was her mom's and not her own. This isn't a slam against high-academic schools; this is a wake-up call to parents who over-orchestrate their kids' lives. But here's the reality: odds are she'll either wind up quitting lacrosse or end up like some of Derek's teammates and transferring. Had she been allowed to make her own decision and been given her parents blessing to do so, the chances would have been far better for a happy outcome—with *her* choice of school and *her* program.

It's important to remember that our children's lives are bigger than sports. The Jennifers of the world will need to make many more life decisions than simply where to go to school. What better way for us, as parents, to help our children make wise choices than by allowing them to lead when it comes to where their athletic success might take them?

After all, it's their life. Not Mom's and Dad's. Unfortunately, too many youth sports parents have missed this lesson along the way.

CHAPTER THREE

SNOWPLOW, DRONE, OR HELICOPTER: (DON'T) PICK YOUR POISON

How overinvolved parents can short-circuit their kids' chance of success

IT WAS CODE-NAMED "OPERATION VARSITY BLUES" after the 1999 comedy. But there was nothing funny about it. In 2019, it was discovered that 33 parents of high school students conspired with other people to use bribery and other forms of fraud to illegally arrange to have their children admitted to top colleges and universities in the U.S.

It was the same "whatever-the-cost" mindset that similarly drives some youth sports parents—only this was on steroids. A number of the cases involved college coaches accepting bribes to see that the adult children of well-to-do families were accepted into the university. The men's tennis coach at the University of Texas, the head coach of the Yale soccer team, an associate athletic director and water polo coach at the University of Southern California—all were among those charged for accepting bribes. Geez, even a Stanford sailing coach—*sailing!*—was involved.

The scam used a multiple-option offense: people taking SAT or ACT tests for high schoolers desiring to attend a particular university. Fake IDs. Cash bribes. Even a sham charity to which parents were encouraged to make donations, one such "donation" being a lofty $6.5 million.

This was a story with an array of pathetic angles, but the saddest part of the tale is that the message the young people got from their parents was: "You aren't capable. You aren't good enough. So, we'll handle this for you." It was more important for the parents to bathe in the prestige of getting their kid into "Brand X" school than for the young person to be allowed to do so on their own merits. Those young people never got the chance to make the attempt on their own.

This, of course, was a case that made national news for months; it involved big money, prestigious universities, and wealthy cheaters, including a few Hollywood actors. But every day, in obscure ways, parents of young athletes, if not cheating per se, are similarly looking for ways to give their children advantages. Parents secure leadership positions within their children's schools so they can overly influence the chances of their kids making a team, getting more playing time, or being a starter. A mother on the Westside of Los Angeles became part of her daughter's middle school volleyball coaching staff to ensure that her child would not only be the starting setter but rarely sit on the bench. Parents lavish coaches with luxury gifts so their child will make the team. Parents hire their child's club coach into corporate jobs to ensure their son will win that starting position. It happens more than you know.

In the volleyball case, the girls quickly sniffed out the ploy and it completely backfired on the mom. The girls who didn't play felt slighted. The daughter who got all the playing time got a bad rap and didn't understand why the girls didn't like her. The other parents went out of their way to ensure that their daughter wouldn't be on this team, not wanting the headaches that came with the mom trying to control everything.

Why did it happen? Because of one snow-plow parent who had lost perspective.

In the Varsity Blues cheating scandal, most parents assumed that their child would never find out about the "little bit of help" they received to get into an elite school, so what harm could it do? But, if they were willing to help with something as large as this, I'm willing to bet there were other areas in their child's development where failure was not an option. It starts when the child is very young, with parents swooping in on homework assignments, finishing projects for them in middle school, and eventually getting a 504 plan for them in time for college board testing in high school. (A 504 plan is intended for students with disabilities, but people with financial means can get their non-disabled child tested and, with doctor approval, get permission to spend more time on the tests.)

My friend's son, Sammy, who took the test in West LA, said, "There were more kids in the 504 classroom than in the regular classroom. In addition to getting extra time, the added benefit is the colleges are blind to anyone who did or didn't get the extra time to take the test. So there is nothing but upside for a kid to be placed in the room where he gets extra time and unfair to those of us who follow the rules by taking the allotted amount of time to finish."

WITH ALL DUE RESPECT, GET OUT OF THE WAY!

When my middle son, Parker, was in first grade, I volunteered to help with the spring party. Eight moms gathered over coffee at a Panera to discuss who was going to organize the games and who was going to bring snacks.

"Who's finished their book report already?" asked one mom.

Confused by the question, I sat back and listened as several other moms discussed how difficult it had been to make the hanging mobile book report and fit all the words on the page the way the teacher wanted. I was shocked that almost all the moms not only knew what the project was but had obviously completed it (for their child).

Completely unaware of the assignment, after school that day I asked Parker, "Do you need to create a book-report diorama?"

He shrugged his shoulders. "Yeah, I think so, I don't know. I haven't read the book yet."

"OK," I responded. "Let me know if you'd like any help talking it through—once you're ready to start."

"Nah, I'm good, Mom," he said. "I got this."

A few weeks later I was in the classroom for back-to-school night and, sure enough, all of the book report mobiles were hanging from the ceiling. Over in the corner was Parker's, with about as much attention applied to it as you would expect from a seven-year-old boy. His words had hurriedly been scribbled in crayon and he'd given zero effort to spell-check his work. Gobs of glue coated the mobile like mountain snow.

I stood there smiling as the teacher, a 30-year veteran, came over to say hello. Obviously, she was reading my mind.

"Some people don't think I can tell who did the work, but I can," she said with a wry smile. "The perfectly typed, double-spaced reports with no spelling errors are pretty much dead giveaways."

What triggers this in parents is an unwarranted fear that their child will fail. When parents want so badly to make sure their child hits the mark—even when the kid is only six or seven— the erosion of their child's confidence begins. The parent may *think* they're being helpful by doing the homework for the child, but the message the child receives is not helpful at all: you don't think they're capable. The child may not begin to put the pieces together until years later, but when they are asked as adults about their confidence and belief in themselves, they might remember an incident as seemingly benign as this. "My mom never thought I was good enough. She started to show me that by doing my first-grade book report—and never stopped."

Ironically, Parker later shared a story from high school he couldn't believe. "In our chemistry class, we had to research some information, write a report, and create a poster board with our findings. My friend Mark's artwork was really good, so I asked him how long he worked on the project. He said, 'Oh, I didn't do the drawing, my mom did.'" Parker couldn't believe it, so he asked his friend if he did the research. "No, my mom likes to do all of that stuff, so I just let her."

So, what does helping your child complete a more perfect assignment in school have to do with youth sports? Everything. The pressure a child feels of having to do perfect schoolwork is the same pressure he feels of having to turn in the perfect athletic performance.

Let your kids' athletic "performances" be their own, even if there undoubtedly will be some globs of glue now and then. Resist the urge to do everything but swing the bat or golf club for them. In short, have enough faith in them to let them fail from time to time.

Affluence and free time are a deadly combination for youth sports parents; they invite overinvolvement from parents in their children's sports lives. Ironically, parents who relentlessly pressure their kids to succeed are doing just the opposite: pressuring their kids to fail. When failure is *not* an option, children pay a price. When parents swoop in to do homework assignments for their kids in grade school and finish projects for them in high school, they are, again, foisting the subconscious message of "you can't handle this on your own, so we have to take over" onto them.

It's far healthier if parents, when their child faces adversity, take a deep breath, ask their child what he or she wants to do, and show some confidence in that child having a say in the matter.

Untangling the Knot of Over-Parenting

So, how can overinvolved parents better deal with situations that might seem unfair to them and, perhaps, to their child?

First, like the fisher who has a knot in her line, the process begins by looking closely at the problem and slowly untangling it—instead of letting emotions trigger knee-jerk reactions.

A client with a son who played soccer called me one day in a cold panic. "I'm not sure what to do," she said. "All of my son's friends are starting to play club and here in Maryland it's very competitive. If he doesn't try out to play club this year, I'm afraid he'll miss the opportunity altogether. Everyone says that if you don't get into the club early, they won't make a team when they are older."

Sounded to me like her middle-school son needed a mom who, for starters, could chill a bit.

"So, how old is your son?"

"Eight."

Had I been drinking coffee, I would have spit it out. Instead, I simply asked her a few questions.

"What are your family's priorities? How much time do you want to spend together on weekends and weekdays? Is it important that he make the top team now or is it OK for him to just have fun playing with a few of his friends on the rec team?"

She assured me that most of his friends were opting for a tryout with the club team, which is what led to her feeling pressure. "If he's not with his friends, he's going to be so upset, I'm afraid he won't want to play anymore. My husband and I both love soccer and we really want him to continue."

I advised her to have a family meeting at which her son could have as much say as anyone else.

"Determine what your priorities are as a family. For example, if you're planning on rafting the river for 10 days this summer, would your sports decision allow for this trip to happen? How important is soccer to him? Would he be just as happy playing rec?"

We spoke a couple weeks later. I was pleased with how far they'd come. They'd decided as a family that they didn't want or need the time commitment of club soccer—yet.

"What about the friends?" I asked. "Does he have any left on the rec team?"

The mother laughed. "He came home from the first rec practice with a huge smile on his face, saying he made at least five new friends."

Sometimes as parents we feel the need to "rush in and rescue" because, in our heads, we've played out the scenario not one step ahead but three years ahead. And it spells doom. *Stop!* Make the decision that works for your family right now. Don't get caught up in keeping up with the Joneses (whoever they are!). If your son's skill and love for the sport continue to grow, he will find the right club as he gets older.

Second, avoid pack-mentality thinking. Parents make too many wrong decisions, frankly, because of peer pressure—yes, even at age 30 or 40 or 50. They look at other parents with the assumption that they must all be right, they must know something you don't know, they are the standard to which you need to conform. *Oh, my gosh, if we don't get on the train now, we'll be forever left behind!* Sure, parents want to provide their children with the best opportunities within reason for the kids to pursue their passion, but where do you draw the line? No down time? No family vacations? No break from the action? Thirteen months a year? ("Well, not quite," I can hear the coach saying. "We'll give you a two-week break in the beginning of May.")

Third, set the tone right from the beginning. For those of you on the front-end of sports parenting with kids ages four and up, start small and focus on fun. I'm a huge advocate for kids playing multiple fun—not super competitive—sports starting at a young age. If a child shows an interest in a sport and asks to play on a team, do your research, discuss as a family if it can work with your schedules, and let your child's preferences lead. Perhaps start with a few camps or clinics just to see if they really like it. Whatever the format looks like for your family, make sure the opportunity to learn includes the Three F's:

- Friends
- Fun
- Fundamentals

Play shouldn't be hypercompetitive. In the early years, children just need to learn the fundamentals of the sport, laugh, and make new friends while participating. They need to enjoy the experience. As a club volleyball coach for 10-year-old girls, it saddens me when chatting with a parent who says her that child is nervous because she's playing for the first time and feels "behind." No 10-year-old should feel as if they can't participate because they haven't tried something yet.

"What other interests does she have?" I'll ask. There are always transferrable skills. In one case, it turned out the girl also took dance lessons and played the flute.

"Wonderful! Then she already knows what it means to be a part of a larger group and work together. She'll pick up skills quickly once she realizes that she is welcomed by her peers—and understands, regardless of her own skill set, that her teammates are just learning, too. Once she gets an introduction to some of the fundamentals most girls jump right in."

Parents shouldn't feel as if they have to apologize if their daughter is only starting the sport at age 10. Many great athletes didn't pick up their "main" sport until their mid-teens. Alex Morgan, a USA soccer gold medal Olympian and two-time FIFA Women's World Cup winner, played multiple sports—volleyball, basketball, and soccer—but didn't join a club team until she was 14.

She attributes a lot of her success to her competitive spirit. She remembers being a competitor at everything she did with her two older sisters. "Beating someone to us was just so sweet, even if it was just a family member." It didn't matter that Alex started competitive soccer at an "older" age because the friends, fun, and fundamentals—combined with her competitive mindset—quickly narrowed the gap. In high school she was an All-American.

Parents who succeed at this youth sports game are parents who prioritize raising healthy kids ready to make their way in the world, rather than kids who are "definitely going to play DI." Research shows that active children become active adults who have lower rates of anxiety and depression and higher rates of self-worth. They also become adults who are more willing to take risks and who have a better understanding of what it takes to be committed to not only themselves but to a team.

Such benefits can be found in both team and individual sports: learning to bounce back from defeats, the results of hard work, the kind of lessons that can help those kids become successful adults, whether the arena is family, careers, or elsewhere.

Sometimes Our Children Teach Us

While researching this book, I met Susan, a parent who embodied the healthy-parenting approach of letting the child drive the sports process once they get to their teen years. Abigail was Susan's third child. They were a military family of six, which meant lots of moves and lots of learning to adjust to new and different circumstances. When Abigail was 14, the family moved from Washington, D.C., to a small, one-high-school town in South Carolina. Abigail loved lacrosse but the school didn't have a team. But what looked at first like a huge disappointment soon turned into a tremendous blessing.

"My husband and I encouraged Abbie to try something new," Susan told me. "So she did. She played basketball and volleyball, she ran track, and she even tried out for the tennis team. The school was so small that the coaches didn't care what level you were; they just needed bodies! She felt welcomed and it gave her a wonderful break from playing lacrosse year-round between her middle school club teams. As parents, we were thrilled. She played for the joy of the sport, without any pressure to make a certain level of team or concern about performing in front of college coaches or overly competitive parents. She could just be a kid. Man, that was fun!"

Alas, her husband's military job demanded a move; when Abigail was a sophomore in high school, he was transferred back to Washington, D.C. But adept at adjusting to change, "She transitioned smoothly back to her Capital Lacrosse Club teammates, almost as if she had never been away," said Susan.

In the spring of 2017, NCAA lacrosse came out with a significant recruiting rule change that banned college lacrosse coaches from communicating with prospective student-athletes (PSAs) until September 1 of their junior year of high school. The ruling came five months after Abbie, then a 16-year-old sophomore, had already committed verbally to playing college lacrosse for a DI school in the East. When recruiting started, she had been excited about the opportunity and flattered that she was being courted by a large school with great academics.

"I didn't exactly know what I wanted to major in at the time; I was just in awe of the campus, impressed by the level of lacrosse and in hindsight, overwhelmed by the recruiting process," she said. "It was a lot for me to take in and it kind of freaked me out. It was a huge relief once I'd said yes to this school."

Her parents had allowed Abbie to make the decision, and she and her parents were happy with the partial scholarship the school offered. All was good—at first. But when the family was invited to attend one of the school's football games when Abbie was a senior, Susan noticed a change in her daughter.

"She just didn't seem herself. She appeared to be just going through the motions of having fun. It wasn't until the following morning when I got the chance to ask her what was going on."

Abbie confessed that she'd been having second thoughts about the school but didn't want to say anything because she didn't want to disappoint her parents or the coach.

"I know both you and Dad and the coach would hate it if I changed my mind and told you I don't want to go to his school."

"Well, hold on a second there!" Susan told her. "First of all, Dad and I are very proud of you. Second of all, this is *your* decision, not ours. Can you tell me a little bit more about why you don't think this is the right school for you?"

Since her sophomore year, Abbie had been an active member of a program at her high school that helped developmentally disabled students. In fact, it was almost as big of a passion for Abbie as lacrosse. Having spent a year working with these students, she realized she really wanted to major in nursing and eventually work with kids with special needs. But the university didn't have the undergrad nursing program she felt she needed.

Great parenting means asking questions and listening to answers—and that's exactly what Susan did.

"So, what do you want to do?" she asked.

"I want to call the coach and tell him I can no longer accept a roster spot and partial scholarship. It's a wonderful offer and a great school; it's just not the right school for *me*. But I feel like it's too late. I'm not allowed to change my mind."

"No, it's not too late," Susan said. "I'd encourage you to be honest with the coach."

Abbie did just that. In the phone call, Abbie told him she couldn't find programs at the school that fit her academic interests because she wanted to major in undergrad nursing—and the school didn't offer it. The coach responded that she shouldn't worry about doing nursing in undergrad, she could do that as a grad student after she finished playing. Then he offered a veiled threat.

"At this late stage in the recruiting season, if you decommit from us, you're never going to be able to play lacrosse at another DI school. Everyone has already given away all of their scholarships."

Abbie was polite but firm. "I understand. And I'm OK with that."

"You're making a big mistake," he told her.

Rather than being awash in guilt, Abbie was invigorated with a new sense of freedom; she felt as if the weight of the world had been lifted off of her shoulders.

"Mom, are you OK if I don't get another offer to play lacrosse?"

"Abbie, we are more than OK. This is your decision. You need to go where you feel like you can not only be successful on the field and in the classroom, but where you are looking forward to the challenge. You have to be happy with your choice of school if for any reason lacrosse doesn't work out."

The lacrosse world is a small one; everyone seems to know everyone. Within a matter of weeks, word got out that Abbie had de-committed from the school. When the lacrosse coach at another DI school called and said he was interested in her and the school *did* have an undergrad nursing program, Abbie had found the best of both worlds.

The moral of the story? While it is so tempting to help solve your child's problems, don't underestimate her ability to do that on her own. As parents, we can be protective; we don't like to see our kids in any discomfort. But the reality is, each of us needs to learn certain lessons for ourselves. And the painful ones are usually the best teachers.

So, to review, be patient and untangle the fishing line. Avoid pack-mentality thinking. Set your tone right from the beginning. And, finally—and most importantly—be the parent who walks alongside her child—without jumping into the hole with them each time they stumble. This will give your kid the confidence to navigate the unknown and find the right path for them.

PART II

STRATEGY I: UNDERSTANDING THE FAST-CHANGING GAME

Chapter Four

PRESSURE VERSUS SUPPORT

Why letting the coach do her thing is often in your child's best interest

AFTER HIS SECOND STRAIGHT TURNOVER, Julian glanced up to the stands and saw his father, whose disappointment was obvious: hands thrown into the air, eyes rolling, head shaking sideways. The boy's eyes said it all: *Sorry, Dad.* Julian looked nervous. His game was off. As one of the smaller ninth graders in this freshman game, he kept turning the ball over, getting stripped, and jacking up ill-advised shots that weren't even close. Nothing was working.

I was sitting next to his father, Joe. Prior to tip-off, I had already gotten an earful: "Man, this has been a frustrating year! This coach stinks! I've already spoken to the varsity coach about Julian. It's a joke. He's barely getting playing time on the freshmen team and everyone knows he should be starting on varsity. Have you watched varsity? Their guards suck."

Actually, I *had* watched the varsity team play as my older son was on the team. In fact, he was one of those "sucky" guards. But the man wasn't really looking for my input, so I let him rumble on like a train about to leave the track.

"Julian was the starting point guard at his middle school last year. Scored 33 points against the best team in the league in playoffs. Unstoppable! We've been having him work out with a trainer who coaches NBA players and the guy told me Julian is a DI player for sure. Why can't this coach see that?"

I said nothing. Now was not a good time to suggest to him that the trainer's priority might well have been clients who paid well. But when he paused, I couldn't resist. "Does Julian know why the coach isn't starting him anymore?"

"He told me, first, he doesn't pass the ball and, second, he doesn't know the plays."

Seemed like pretty good reasons to put someone on the bench, not that the father shared my unspoken perspective. "What does that matter?" he said. "He's the best player on the floor. They aren't letting him do his thing."

My heart hurt for Julian. He was a quick, agile athlete. His dad was right; in past years his athleticism meant he could score the ball, but now, going up against taller opponents, it was tougher for him to find good shots. His dad had enjoyed the last five or six years of watching his son dominate at the grade-school and middle-school levels. But now 5'6", Julian was a sapling in an old-growth forest. And with a father who was perhaps 5'8" and a mother who was 5'5", the chances of Julian being a DI athlete weren't great, meaning if ever he needed that "being coachable" wrench in his toolbox, this was it.

The problem? His father not only couldn't find the tool, he didn't know it existed. It's not uncommon to find parents who can't see the forest for the trees. Despite all of his good intentions, Joe had made a few critical coaching errors in his attempt to help Julian become the best high school basketball player he could be. Despite having limited info on this father-son relationship, experience suggested post-game conversations like this:

Son: "Dad, I'm so frustrated I'm not starting anymore! Coach isn't playing me because he says I don't know the plays and am not passing the ball."

Father: "You're the best player out there. This is ridiculous. I know the varsity head coach. I'm going to call him and sort this out. You're doing nothing wrong. Keep doing what you're doing."

Son: "Are you sure that's a good idea, Dad? Maybe that will make my coach mad."

Father: "I don't care what your coach says, he doesn't know what he's doing. You're better than most of the guards on varsity. You should be playing varsity, not riding the freshman bench! This is ridiculous. When you get in, don't listen to your coach; just take control and drive to the basket. You're a scorer. You just need to do your thing."

Joe's heart was in the right place. Clearly, he loved watching his son play basketball. But he failed to do three things that would have helped the young man succeed:

- **Give him space.** Parents, this is your children's journey, not yours. If things shift and they go from starters to reserves, ask them what *they* are going to do about it. Encourage them to speak to the coach. And then, zip it! As hard as it is, keep your mouth shut and let your son or daughter look for their own solutions. They are being battle-tested. They will either come out defeated because you intervened and took control of the situation or will struggle but find their own path. Regardless of the outcome, your kids need to learn that they are capable of figuring out what the coach is looking for, making mental and physical adjustments, and learning along the way.

- **Listen to the feedback.** Whatever feedback your children receive, you need to ask them how they feel about it. In Julian's case, does it make sense that as the point guard he should pass the ball more and learn the plays? *Of course!* That's what point guards do. Give the coach the benefit of the doubt. Even if your son is the best player out there, what skill sets can he add to his game now? Because if he wants to play JV or eventually varsity, the game is only going to get faster, the boys stronger, and the need for smart ball-distributors all the more critical. If he's still riding a fat-tire Schwinn as guys zoom by on carbon-fiber bicycles, he's doomed. He needs to change tools and adapt perspectives. And if you were his parent, you need to help him understand that "changing his game" is going to be to his, and the team's, benefit.

- **Bite your tongue.** As difficult as it is for us to watch our kids hit speed bumps, the gift they will receive is on the other side of the pain. Don't deny them the beauty of learning a life lesson. So, it's not working. What can the young athlete do about it? Brainstorm—without providing answers—ideas about how they might get more playing time. For example, in Julian's case, he might try going through a practice disciplining himself to *not* shoot—to show the coach what he can do and how he can put the team first. Or directly asking the coach or one of his teammates to help him better learn the plays. Collaboration and asking for feedback may emerge as his greatest asset in showing his coach and teammates that he's "in it to win it" with the team. If he has been a shoot-first point guard, his teammates might have stopped expecting to ever see the ball, which dilutes their individual performances, the team's overall game, and the players' trust in him.

Granted, the pattern of Joe encouraging Julian to "just take over" probably didn't start this season, so it will be a challenging habit to break. But a dad who is interested in seeing his son learn and grow should also be looking at how he, too, can learn and grow as a parent.

Sadly, none of this—or the three lessons—happened in the Joe–Julian relationship. By the final game of the year, Joe rarely came to Julian's games because he was so angry at his son's lack of playing time. It was obviously a confusing and painful time for Julian. What does it say to a child when his father stops coming to his games? This: *My love for you is conditional. I will only support you when you soar, not when you struggle.* You could argue that the latter occasion is when a parent needs to be *especially* supportive.

Meanwhile, as this father was, in essence, quitting on his son, the team put together a winning season. Most players grew and developed a lot over the months. At the team banquet, there was only one player and family not in attendance. It broke my heart, as we left, to see the poster-sized photo that Joe had ordered early in the season—sitting alone on the checkout table.

Finding Joy on the Court—or on the Bench

When meeting Greg Paulus, Niagara University men's basketball coach, you wouldn't have guessed that that he was a two-sport DI athlete who ran point for perennial basketball powerhouse Duke for four years (2005–2009) and later was the starting quarterback for Syracuse (2009–2010). A former Mr. Basketball for the state of New York and the Gatorade Player of the Year, he stands at 6'1", and is maybe 180 pounds, soaking wet; in other words, hardly a dominating specimen in the game of college hoops. Yet, in 2005, he was the No. 1 high school basketball recruit in the country.

How did that happen? He must have had parents who really pushed him to get to that level, right?

"Actually, it was quite the opposite," said Paulus, one of seven kids in the family. "Being raised in upstate New York, my parents encouraged us all to pursue our passions but there was never an expectation that we'd play a sport in college." All four of Greg's older brothers attended Georgetown University. The oldest, David, played both basketball and football there. And many assumed Greg, too, would become a Hoya on the Hilltop.

"That doesn't mean we weren't a competitive family. In fact, I think some of the most intense competitions I've ever been a part of were trying to beat my older brothers in *anything*. The family game of choice was ping-pong. According to my dad, I was the fourth-best player in my house. One thing he's is very proud of is his ping-pong record."

Despite being extremely competitive amongst family members, it was always in good fun and never to belittle or demoralize someone else—something that served him well during his Duke career. He was a pass-first point guard who embraced his role and helped lead the team as a freshman to win the Atlantic Coast Championship (ACC) in 2005. He started both his sophomore and junior years as well, but his senior year, the starting spot was won by sophomore Nolan Smith.

How did Greg respond to the setback? According to legendary Duke coach Mike Krzyzewski, "Like a pro." He accepted that his new role, in order to help Duke win, was to come off the bench and make the biggest impact he could. And that's exactly what he did, even though he got only 16 minutes of playing time—less than half a game—the entire season.

Did he quit? Go through the motions? Sulk? Nope. "Many people don't know this about him, but he was the hardest worker out there," his father, Dave, said. "Always the first one in the gym and the last to leave."

Being the fifth of seven children, Greg recalls a childhood filled with love, laughter, and an intense desire to get better at whatever challenge presented itself. If he beat one of his four older brothers—he also had one younger brother and a younger sister—it was a big night at the dinner table. "My parents never focused on winning or getting on the top team; they just opened the door and let us race out to play. We created the competition."

Obviously, Greg's parents did well as the potters of the clay they were given. Here are some of the values Greg says he learned growing up in a family of nine—values he now uses as a DI head coach and as a father of two:

- **Encourage your kid to work hard and be a good teammate.** Greg always valued the gift of being able to support his teammates, realizing that doing that would make the team better as a whole. It was never about his needing to be the star; it was about embracing whatever role he had, whether it was a starter as a freshman or coming off the bench as a senior. "It didn't really bother me that much. Of course, I wanted to be on the floor, but I trusted Coach K's opinion and it meant I needed to work harder to get as much playing time as I could."

- **Lean back.** As parents, there is a fine line between being supportive and being controlling. Parents can help by laying out the buffet of sports options for their child to choose from. But once the kid has selected a path, the choice shouldn't feel as if it has been dictated to him. It shouldn't feel as if it has to be taken to the highest level, "or else!" When pressure overtakes curiosity, fear sets in and the athlete eventually implodes. Either a. the subliminal pressure gets too great and he opts out altogether, or b. the fear of disappointing the only true opinion that seems to matters, their parents', becomes too much to bear and quitting feels safer than trying to navigate the fear of the unknown.

- **Find gratitude.** Focus on the gifts that your child has. This opens up the possibility for more options to "come their way." To focus on, say, the shortcoming of a coach is to burden your child with is the weight of impossibility. Parents who support, rather than pressure, their kids, focus on the attributes the child already has. "You outwork everyone on the court." "You have a great attitude and, more importantly, the desire to get better." "No, you didn't score but your pass was the key to our entire comeback."

Whether the topic is sports or school or life in general, what are the characteristics you want your child to embody? Focus on those; find ways to encourage your child in relation to those values. Talent, you see, only takes a young athlete so far. For example, here are 10 things that are extremely valuable to an athlete but require no talent at all:

- Work ethic
- Being on time
- Effort
- Body language
- Energy
- Attitude
- Passion
- Being coachable
- Doing extra
- Being prepared

Reward your kid when he or she displays such qualities; you'd be surprised at how rich the return on your investment will be. At practice or during games, your child might not get much encouragement, even if a coach might appreciate hustle, passion, and preparation. So, do what you can to help your kids create the best versions of themselves possible. In the process, they can teach us, too, if we allow them to.

And isn't that the win-win we should be looking for?

CHAPTER FIVE

WHEN LIFE GIVES YOU LEMONS...

*Modeling the values of good sportsmanship,
fair play, and hard work*

MORE THAN 50 YEARS AFTER THE INCIDENT, an older friend of mine still remembers it. Now 68, he was only 10 when he'd failed miserably during a Punt, Pass, & Kick football competition. Everywhere he looked, his buddies were proudly holding up their blue, red, and white ribbons with pride. Dejected, he headed out of the high school stadium to meet his mother for the ride home.

"Hey, Jimmy," he heard from behind him.

He turned to see one of the officials, the father of one of his friends.

"We have one more award to hand out—and it's actually for you. Here." The man handed the boy a spanking-new orange kicking tee. "It's the sportsmanship award. And you're the winner. You had a tough day, but you encouraged your pals and never complained. Good for you!"

More than a half century later, the man all but tears up when telling the story.

"At the time, being only 10, I didn't see what was really going on—the man felt sorry for me and invented an award to take away some of the hurt. But, in the big-life picture, what he did was turn what could have been a negative experience into a positive one. And I've never forgotten that lesson: that sports are about more than winning. They're about deeper things—in this case, sportsmanship."

As a parent, your child is looking to you to help them navigate the often rocky world of youth sports—and life itself. And at times that's going to involve finding ways to turn what look to be negative situations into positive ones.

And that won't always be easy. Why? Because our brains are wired for negativity bias. What that Punt, Pass, & Kick official did was take what could have been a negative situation and help make it positive. But in doing so, he cut against the grain of a human natural tendency.

"It is our tendency not only to register negative stimuli more readily but also to dwell on these events," writes Kendra Cherry in *The Everything Psychology Book (2nd Edition)*. "Also known as positive-negative asymmetry, this negativity bias means that we feel the sting of a rebuke more powerfully than we feel the joy of praise."

As humans, we tend to:

- Remember traumatic experiences better than positive ones.
- Recall insults more readily than praise.
- React more strongly to negative stimuli.
- Think about negative things more frequently than positive ones.
- Respond more strongly to negative events than to equally positive ones.

The Amazing Resiliency of Children

My then 14-year-old daughter, Kylie, who was relatively calm and understated for a teenage girl, came flying in the front door after a volleyball qualifier tournament.

"The ref was *soooooo* bad in the last match! We lost the game because of her, 13–15 in the third."

"How did the other two matches go?" I asked.

"Oh, those were fine. We won those. But our team is so mad about the last game!"

She offered an unusually detailed description of every bad call the referee made in the apparently dreadful final game.

In that moment, my daughter was reacting to a negative situation and allowing it to overshadow the positive—that they'd actually won two other matches, for example. Imagine, then, what can happen when, as parents, we amplify our child's negativity by "going negative" ourselves. By calling the ref's association or confronting a coach who isn't playing our kid enough or whining about our kid being cut. Instead, for example, using what looks like, at first glance, a negative situation and turning it into something positive.

Michelle, the daughter of a friend, started playing rec soccer for American Youth Soccer Organization (AYSO) soccer when she was eight. By 10, she was enjoying the sport so much her parents decided it was a good time for her to try out for a more competitive soccer team. She went through the tryouts for Santa Monica United and was excited for the opportunity to practice more regularly and compete against stronger soccer players. But when the final team roster was announced, only one player's name from the previous season's AYSO team wasn't on the list: Michelle's.

"I want to quit!" she told her parents.

Her father, Todd, who had played college football at the University of Oregon, didn't do what a lot of parents would have done: saddle up to ride to her rescue by confronting the coach. Instead, he calmly sat down with his daughter.

"How long have you been playing soccer, Michelle?"

She shrugged her shoulders. "Dunno. Two years?"

"How long do you think some of these girls who made the team have been playing?"

Second shoulder shrug. "Dunno. Two years?"

"Jill's been playing for four years and Samantha for five. That's more than double the time you've been playing. What do you think that means in terms of how much better they could be?"

Another shoulder shrug. "Dunno. Guess it means I stink. I'm gonna quit."

Todd knew something that Michelle didn't. He'd been a late bloomer. He didn't start playing football until high school and still earned a DI college scholarship. He had what most children—and too many parents—don't have: perspective. He saw the big picture, the "long game," the nuances that suggested what his daughter did in sports from ages six to eight wasn't going to be nearly as important as two other things: how much she might grow to love the game as she matured and how willing she might be to work hard and get better.

But did you see what he did in leaning toward a solution? By asking his daughter the questions, by trusting her to see a bigger picture, by giving her the freedom to contribute to a solution, he was empowering her to be more—not just as an athlete, but as a human being.

While his heart hurt for his daughter and, instinctively, he might have wanted to "make it all better" right now, his head told him: *be patient*. Even if she wouldn't get to play with all of her friends who'd made the team, it was going to be OK. As a parent, the better play wasn't rattling the coach's cage but helping his daughter get onto a team where she could learn, grow, and deepen her passion for the game.

And that's exactly what he did. Michelle continued to play soccer for another AYSO team. She made new friends and learned lots from the new coach.

Flash forward five years. At 15, Michelle tried out for club soccer once again—ironically, for a team coached by the same person who had cut her at age 10. When announcing the roster, the coach suddenly paused.

"This is something that has never happened in my 20-plus years of coaching," he told the group of players and parents. "I cut this player five years ago. Most times when kids get cut, I never see them again. They quit. This player did not. She obviously decided to work hard on her game—and I'm so excited to offer her a roster spot this year. I think she is going to be one of our strongest players and has the potential to become a true leader on and off the field. Congratulations and welcome, Michelle!"

As people broke into applause, Michelle beamed. This was her "kicking-tee" moment. Just as my friend never forgot how his negative Punt, Pass, & Kick experience turned into something positive, I'm betting Michelle will never forget how she turned what was a dark point in her youth into something far brighter. And how graciously her coach affirmed her effort.

Look, we are a society that craves instant gratification. We want what we want, and we want it *now*. If we don't get it in the moment, we move on, often with an abundance of vengeance and a lack of perspective. But next time your daughter doesn't get what she wants in sports, don't panic and press the "protect, protect, protect" button. Instead, welcome it as an opportunity for short-term pain that can reap long-term gain. Ask yourself, what is best for your daughter, not only right now, but more importantly, in the long run. When she doesn't immediately get the outcome she desires, what do you want her to learn about how to respond?

Learning how to delay gratification might be one of the best life skills she acquires. In a sense, you're testing her, trusting her, asking her: *How badly do you want this?* If you don't stand firm and give her the chance to dig deeper and develop some grit, she won't. Because what brings that out in a child isn't having everything handed to her on a silver platter, but *resistance:* having to overcome an obstacle in her path. In essence, it's the same stuff that might make her great on the field—overcoming the resistance of an opponent, circumstances, maybe even hard-to-deal with teammates and coaches. But this is how she will become grittier and stronger over time. It's the same theory that helps an athlete get stronger: you lift more weights (resistance), you swim more laps (resistance), you sprint more 50s (resistance). Whatever you do, you translate the pressure working *against you* into something working *for you.*

Angela Duckworth, in her *New York Times* best-selling book, *Grit: The Power of Passion and Perseverance,* defines grit as a combination of passion and perseverance for a singularly important goal. A key determiner of how your kid will handle future disappointment is: What happens when she *doesn't* get what she wants at first, whether it's a grade on a test or making a team or learning a new skill? Does she sulk, bellyache, quit? Does she allow a perceived setback to keep her "playing small?" Or does she use that opportunity to get curious, ask questions, learn more, and figure out what it's going to take to make the top team? In other words, does she "play big?"

Sometimes Less Is More

Parents—and I am one, so I am speaking to myself, too—don't take this the wrong way, but here's a reality you need to face: sometimes less (of you) is more. At least for your kid. Sometimes you need to step back. Sometimes you need to put less stress on yourself to solve a problem involving your kid and sports—and more trust in your kid to do the same.

Kathy Lietzke, director of finance and recruiting for the Austin Junior Volleyball club in Texas, reminded me of exactly this. We were talking about how COVID-19 protocols had forced the club to make changes in its program, a major one being not allowing parents in the gym to watch tryouts for the upcoming club volleyball season. (The state's COVID regulations wouldn't allow that many people in the gym.)

"And how did that change tryouts for the athletes?" I asked.

"It was a huge relief for them," she said. "The kids are used to having to perform not only for the coaches but also for their parents, who question them the entire ride home about not only how they played but what team they think they will make. This time, the kids were able to just play and not worry about looking over their shoulder at Mom or Dad."

As they went through the multi-day tryout, the coaches assessed where each player in each age group best fits. Kids develop at different rates. Sometimes, for example, a girl hits puberty early and is 5'10" at age 12—but is uncoordinated and awkward on the court, totally lost. But because of her height, she will be given a spot on a higher-level team with hopes that she'll grow into her body over time and gain coordination along the way. Sometimes this hunch by the coaches is right; she grows into her body and that latent athleticism emerges. On the other hand, if the following year of this "experiment" finds her still struggling, a good coaching staff will realize she is better off on a lower-level team so she can gain confidence, develop basic skills, and be better prepared to play at a higher level down the road.

In the past, Lietzke told me, whenever the Austin coaches, during a tryout, would see a player who needed to be moved down a level, they would tap on her shoulder and ask her to come to a back room where her parents would join in the discussion. Everyone in the gym knew exactly what was happening—and avoided being tapped on the shoulder as if it were the plague.

But with no parents in the gym, the result—to the surprise of the coaches—was far different. The girls handled the situation with refreshing maturity. When a coach tapped the shoulder of 16-year-old Chrissy, she knew exactly what was coming.

"Would you rather wait to have this discussion with your parents?" a coach asked her.

"Nope, I got this," she quickly responded.

The coaches explained that she was going to be moved down to the second team. She handled it brilliantly instead of spiraling into a death spin of self-pity or anger. "It makes sense. I totally get it. Can I go back out there and keep playing now?"

For better *and* worse, the staff knew Chrissy's parents well and, after the young player left, looked at each other with stunned expressions of disbelief.

"Wow, that would have gone entirely differently had her parents been in the room," said a coach. Everyone nodded, eyes wide.

Her parents had been known to make a fuss, pushing for her to not only be on the top team but getting maximum playing time once she was on that team. Now, Chrissy seemed quietly thrilled to not be caught in the crossfire of her parents pushing the coaches for more playing time—and free to enjoy the sport she loved at a level that was better suited for her developmentally.

When Coach Lietzke shared this story with me, it resonated. As a former DI volleyball player (William & Mary), I could empathize with the stress Chrissy felt. Kylie, then 14, had just started playing volleyball two years earlier. Being late to the sport, she wasn't one of the stronger players on her team last year. In fact, she was one of those taller girls who got moved up based more on her height and potential than on her ability. When COVID-19 forced a shift in protocol, it was, in a strange way, a nice reprieve for her.

Let me explain: despite her height, Kylie lacked the skill development to keep up with her peers on the top team. She was struggling to get onto the court at all during tournaments, which I could tell was frustrating for her. Once the season was called off due to COVID-19 in mid-March 2020, her coach conducted workouts via Zoom six days a week. Because people were no longer allowed to get together in person, the coaches would have kids log onto a Zoom call and each kid would do the workout in their own backyard. Rather than use this as an excuse to lose interest in the game, Kylie responded positively—on her own. Now being "behind" developmentally no longer mattered. What was going to matter was how seriously each girl took the opportunity to get better with what she was given. She dedicated herself to the Zoom workouts and not only did what the coaches asked of her, but more—on her own.

In a limited capacity, the team returned to the court for a few tournaments the following season. And Kylie started getting more playing time. Why? Because she had decided on her own to put in the hard work—and it paid off.

I admit, however, that it wasn't easy for me to stay out of the way. I struggled with how best to support her. My top priority is for her to have fun, enjoy the game, and not worry about the crowd. I want her to play because *she* loves it. Period. I don't want her to feel any pressure to play volleyball because her mom did. If it's not her thing, I'm good with that.

All of which sounds awesome in theory. However, when I learned that parents, with COVID-19 restrictions loosened, were being allowed to attend an upcoming tournament, it forced me to put that theory in play.

"Please be honest," I said to her. "Would you rather I *not* come? Does it feel like too much pressure?"

She looked me dead in the eye. "Mom, it's up to you. You can come if you like. But, yes, I do feel a bit more pressure when you are there."

Ouch. Pressure is the last thing I wanted her to feel. And, by the way, it was pressure for me, too. Full disclosure: I'm a ridiculously competitive person, so it was hard for me to watch the previous year when she wasn't getting much playing time. For the first time ever, I was completely able to empathize with some of my clients who share about their kids riding the bench. At times, I wanted to go nose-to-nose with that coach and say, "Please give my kid a chance!" But my "inner life coach" came out and I quietly reassured myself that things were playing out just as they were supposed to.

I advise my clients when they are upset at their kids' games to do one of three things: "Sit on your hands, distract yourself by talking to the parent next to you about something completely unrelated, or if you really can't handle it, go for a walk." That season, I'll admit it, I did all three.

In the end, just as COVID had a silver lining in Austin when it came to youth volleyball, so did it in LA, where I live. With parents barred from attending games, Kylie and I both found it a relief. She relaxed, got better, gained confidence, and began enjoying volleyball more. I took pride in how she'd come up with a solution on her own—and, frankly, enjoyed having a bit more "down time," and watched the matches over Zoom from home.

Sometimes the best thing we can do as parents is *get out of the way!* Let her play her sport, have fun with it, and give you the full update when she gets home each night.

Apparently, in the last match, the ref really did suck. She told me all about it—and it was fun to hear it through her eyes. So, don't prop yourself up as the sage on the stage. Instead, quietly guide from the side.

THREE WAYS TO LET GO

The lessons to take from this?

- **First, recognize your "natural negativity bias."** We all tend to do it—focus on the negative instead of the positive. So, no, you're not going to overcome this one overnight. But psychologists say we should shower our children with three positive strokes for every negative stroke we offer. That doesn't mean, however, riding to the rescue every time your child gets dealt a bad hand. Instead, help your kid through that moment while offering long-range perspective. That will build trust between the two of you and encourage your child to realize she can overcome obstacles on her own.

- **Second, allow your kid to develop her grit.** Your child will become stronger in her convictions if you support her through the times she doesn't get what she wants. Those are the best life lessons so, counterintuitive as it might seem, *don't* do whatever it takes to make the hurt go away. Instead, bend such situations to your child's advantage. Life isn't always fair, and even if you might think you're being cruel at the time, force yourself to be guided by "big life" principals. They might not bear fruit for some time, but, in the long game, will prove far more valuable to your kid than always trying to shield her from hurt. I like to say "short-term losses for long-term gains." So you lost the game or didn't get much playing time to start; focus on what you can control right now, today, and move in the direction of your goals.

- **Third, embrace that ever-so-rare "COVID silver lining" that suggests getting out of the way might be just what your kid needs.** You don't *always* need to be there. Your children are more resilient than you might give them credit for. They need time and space to grow. And when you do that, you grow too.

Chapter Six

ROLE MODEL OR WRECKING BALL?

When good intentions lead to bad actions and negative consequences

In the skies above Briarcliff, Pennsylvania, the plane circled for 30 minutes over the baseball diamond on that glorious sunny day in May 2018. At first, people weren't quite sure what to make of it. Was it really possible that the banner was targeted at coaches of the Briarcliff High School baseball team? It seemed so. Its message was as simple as it was mean-spirited: Fire coaches Schrader & Kowalczyk.

The team must have been having a lousy season, right? Nope. The team was 18–3 and the two coaches, John Schrader and assistant Walter Kowalczyk, were generally well regarded. But apparently one group of parents, whose sons weren't getting enough playing time, disagreed. And they paid more than $1,200 to vent their frustration.

If Chapter 5 was about youth sports parents who occasionally drive just over the speed limit and need to slow down, this chapter is about parents who think, "Speed limit? What's a speed limit?" This is for folks who need desperately to slow down and understand the long-term detrimental effects their out-of-control behavior can have on their children. Or to have someone take the keys from them and refuse to let them drive.

Decades ago, the banner-in-the-sky story would have sold as fiction. No one would have believed parents would waste hard-earned money to humiliate coaches, particularly ones who were so well thought of in the community. But in today's professionalized youth sports era, such behavior is not only *not* far-fetched, but more commonplace than it should be. On our *#RaisingAthletes* podcast, Susie Walton and I hear them all the time: stories from wigged-out sports parents engaged in a sort of how-low-can-you-go limbo regarding bad behavior.

The parents who transferred their 7'0" son to four different high schools in three states because they believed the basketball program wasn't doing enough to help him get recruited.

The woman who is discouraging her teenage kids from playing sports altogether because she can't get the feeling of complete dejection out of her head from the memory back at age 14 when her father pulled the car over on the side of the freeway, told her how disgusted he was with her, and made her walk five miles home after losing a tennis match.

The countless parents who spend the entire car ride home berating their child for what they did wrong in the game and how it lost the game for the team (too many versions of this to count!).

Dillon and the Overzealous Father

Several years ago, when our middle child, Parker, was just learning soccer, my husband, Evan, had just settled into his beach chair to watch a game. That's when it happened.

Dillon! Run, Dillon!

The father, just down from Evan, yelled so loudly my husband almost spilled his coffee. But that was just the opening act.

Up and down the field, Dillon ran.

Up and down the field, the dad followed.

Up and down the field, Dillon tried to concentrate on the task at hand, zigging and zagging in a frenzied, if chaotic, attempt to apparently please his father.

Up and down the field, Dad persisted in trying to control his son as if the kid were a remote-control car, not a child. Forward. Backward. Left. Right. All the time, the father barking instructions. The. Entire. Game.

So appalled was Evan that he mentioned the man's behavior—and the kid's frenetic response—to another parent after the game.

"Yeah, we played baseball with that family a few years ago," the dad casually observed. "Dillon's dad said he'd drop a little Adderall into his son's cereal in the morning before the tee ball games because he couldn't stand to watch him 'picking grass' and not paying attention in the outfield." Adderall, of course, is a prescription drug that helps with attention deficit hyperactivity disorder (ADHD).

Evan just shook his head.

Wrecking Ball or Role Model?

Our son CJ's Amateur Athletic Union (AAU) basketball team was competing in a national tournament in Las Vegas in front of a handful of college coaches. It was a small gym with not many bleachers, so parents from both teams were all sitting together in one group. A parent from the other team—he'd been particularly vocal near the top of the stands—apparently decided he needed to get closer to the action. He moved to the front row so he could heckle the referee every single time she ran up and down the floor.

At first it was just mild grunts and groans. But as the game went on and his son's team fell further behind, the father started yelling at the players and the refs. He didn't restrict his obscenities to what he thought qualified as bad calls. Nothing was off-limits for the ref who was closest to the bleachers: from her skin color to her weight and to how out of shape he thought she was.

Look; at times, we all blow it. In our zeal to support our children in youth sports, we say something or do something that crosses the line. But there's a difference between an emotional outburst that we later regret and being a serial jackass without an ounce of remorse or regret.

So, where do you draw the line between enthusiastically supporting your kids and becoming an embarrassment? How do you be a role model and not a wrecking ball? First, let's address how you're guaranteed to be an embarrassment to your kid: Wrecking Ball:

- **During games, yell constantly.** Your child can become intimidated if he always hears you yelling, either at him or at the refs. A quick test to gauge whether you've been guilty of this is the answer to this question: Where does your child look after most plays? If it's at you in the stands or on the sidelines, that's bad news. He should be dialed into instructions or encouragement from the coach, not being distracted by whether you approve of his play or the ref's calls. If you're chatter elicits constant looks from your kid, you're overstepping your sports-parent bounds. You're not helping him, you're hurting him.

- **Don't practice what you preach.** If you tell your child to be respectful during the game but act disrespectfully yourself, how do you think your child is going to act? Kids can smell hypocrisy from a mile away. Chances are, they're going to ignore your encouragement to behave and are going to act like you act. And who can blame them? In short, if you encourage your kid to be a positive force, then walk the talk yourself.

- **Pretend your kid is a professional athlete.** At sporting events, our culture allows for profanity and craziness far beyond what's normal in everyday society. Think pro wrestling, pro football, or hockey. Seeing someone on TV screaming at the top of their lungs at the refs or opposing team is commonplace. But that's not appropriate behavior for a kids' sporting event. Never mind that youth sports have been tainted with their own "win-at-all-costs" mentality, there's no place for actions that demean or belittle the players, coaches, refs, or parents. Remember who these young people are: *kids*.

Role Model:

- **Behave.** Cheer when a great play is made by *either* team. Nothing means more to an athlete than having a parent from the opposing team come up to them after the game and say, "Wow! It was fun to watch you play. What's your name? I want to remember to watch out for you in a few years. Keep working hard!"

- **Cheer for everyone on your child's team, not just your son or daughter.** And limit your comments to saying positive things like, "Go Panthers!" (Or whatever the mascot is.) "Great work!" And don't always save your enthusiasm for the girl with the killer spike or the running back who scores all the touchdowns. Applaud teamwork, hustle, and the like. "Beautiful assist!" is just as good as "Great shot!"

- **Step back to gain perspective.** Try and watch the game through the unbiased observer's eyes or the coach's eyes. (I know, I know, not easy!) An unbiased observer will be looking for opportunities to see the great play on both sides. If you tend to get heated about playing time, for example, evaluate why the coach might be playing the entire team in a close game—because it's early in the season and giving minutes to everyone helps build the trust and confidence in all players. While the parent stresses about the loss, the coach knows that early in the season is a great time for the team to bond and grow—even if it might mean an occasional loss in the process. Short-term pain for long-term gain. The kind of thing that perspective helps you see.

- **Remember: monkey see, monkey do.** Our kids learn far more by what we *show* them than by what we *tell* them. Consider your mom's tried-and-true adage about the amount of time you should spend listening versus speaking, "You have two ears and one mouth, so you should listen twice as much as you speak." Spend way more time modeling good behavior than explaining to your kids what good behavior looks like.

- **Zip it.** As much as we think we might have something useful to add after the game about our kid's performance or their attitude, keep quiet. Win or lose, your kid is going to be emotional right after a game. And so are we. Say nothing for the first 10 minutes in the car unless it's clear she wants to talk about her performance. If she says nothing, you can ask her if she'd like to hear what you think. If she says yes, use that time to compliment her, even if only for the one thing she did right in a game filled with frustrating "wrongs." "I loved seeing you cheering on your teammates after you came out. I know it wasn't the game you wanted to have." Wait for a day or so to ask if you can offer any suggestions. You'll both be seeing clearer then and if your child is like most teenagers, she will have moved on entirely by then. If we're critical of our child right after a game, we're building into that young person a dangerous message, intended or not: as a parent, my love for you is not unconditional but dependent on your performance.

I have one young client who, after she's played a game, admits to looking for a friend to walk out of the gym with after a loss.

"My dad yells at me the entire way home and I know it's coming, so I like to try and at least get five minutes of quiet to prepare for it."

That's just sad. The only thing sadder is thinking about the kids on the Pennsylvania baseball team who had to live with the shame of parents who berated their coaches with a plane-towed banner.

We not only can do better than this; for the sake of our children, we must.

CHAPTER SEVEN

ENJOYING THE RIDE

*Creating an environment for your kid to feel loved
and supported (no matter the day's outcome)*

THE RESTAURANT'S MASHED POTATOES WERE cold and the roast beef a tad dry, but the athletes and their families were nonetheless happy to gather and celebrate a moderately successful high school basketball season in Western New York on this March evening in 2014. Representing varsity, JV, and eighth-ninth-grade teams, the boys sat in nervous anticipation about what their coach might say about them. They slouched at their tables, embarrassed about their lopsided ties, two-inches-too-short chinos, and wrinkly, button-down shirts, most certainly grabbed from the far reaches of their closets. The only thing they were comfortable with were the Nikes on their feet, which they lived in.

The discomfort only got worse. As was customary, after dinner the varsity coach took to the podium and said a few kind words about the season and the team. Then each senior was given an opportunity to come to the podium in front of the hundred-plus people and say what their basketball careers had meant to them. As the mother of a then-eighth-grade player, I was envisioning what my son might say as a senior. Suddenly, I was jolted back to the present by something the first senior said.

"I'd like to thank my mom and dad for taking me to practices and games," he began, "but most of all I'd like to thank my sister because she was the one whose shoulder I would cry on once I got home from a game we lost. I always dreaded the car ride home. Dad would chew me out the entire way and she was always there to support me."

Nothing about his team winning the third-grade championship. Nothing about the coach who believed in him in middle school. Nothing about what his parents' support meant to him. Instead, what he remembered most about his childhood basketball experience was the awful car rides home.

Relax, I told myself. *Among the three seniors, surely, he's an anomaly—a kid with a sad story but not representing the experience the others had had.* Boy was I wrong. I was stunned to hear the two others share similar stories about what they remembered most about basketball: their car ride homes with demanding parents. Each couched his remarks in humor, but you could feel the pain beneath. I left the banquet that night shaken by what I'd heard, saddened by their remarks, wondering what their deeper stories were. I had to admire them for their honesty and, frankly, their courage. But I grieved for all three.

The Uncomfortable Drives Home

As parents, we all lose our cool occasionally. And we all have desire to see our children succeed. That can translate into being too hard on our kids on occasion. But do you see what can happen when that becomes our default format? It can become a detriment to our kid that he'll remember the rest of his life.

Example, before you've even shifted the car from neutral to drive: "Why did you pass the ball to Brian? We *all* know that Brian can't shoot and he's a total ball hog. You should have just taken the last shot yourself!"

It may be cathartic to unload on your kid, but what you're actually doing in such cases is putting someone else down (a teammate) at your child's expense. It's a two-for-one no-no that might seem appropriate to you but sends a subliminal message to your child: *If I fail, I will disappoint my parents.*

Will that help your child be a better athlete? No. Because the next time he's in that situation, what he doesn't need to be thinking is: *How will my decision on the court affect my father?* What he needs to be thinking is: *What play gives our team the best chance to succeed—me passing or shooting?*

More importantly, will that help your child be a better human being? No. Because children thrive when they know they are loved unconditionally—and struggle when sensing that they always have to *prove their worth.*

When what you perceive to be failure on your kid's part gets replaced by your own ego's need to win, everyone loses. We all crave to know that we are enough just as we are—and we crave to know that from the people we love and respect the most.

One of my father's favorite sayings was, "You only have today. You might as well enjoy the ride!" I'll admit as a young child I didn't quite get it, but when I became a parent myself 22 years ago, the saying quickly became part of my vernacular as well. We can't always control what happens to us, but we have 100 percent control of how we respond to it. Before doing or saying anything, check in with yourself by asking what your younger self would want to hear, and respond with your kid's best interest in mind.

LETTING KIDS FIND THE ANSWERS

Melissa, a mother of two and former college classmate of mine who now lives in a Washington, D.C., suburb, reached out to me, seeking advice about how to help navigate club soccer for her 10-year-old. I could tell from the sound of her voice that she was rattled, unsure how to respond to what had just transpired.

"My younger son, Joey, has been on the top team on our area's travel soccer program," she began. "Following three days of tryouts, we just got word last night that he has been offered a spot on the *second* team for next year. I haven't told him yet because I didn't want to upset him before he left for school this morning. I'm just heartsick for him. I'm trying to play it cool and be the 'moderated parent,' but am having to check all kinds of emotions, including:

Why the hell do we do this at age 10?

Really, he starts for the top team for two years and **now** *he's on the second team?*

Who the F cares?

My kid's the best and I'd like to rip the coach's face off.

All expressed in jest. Sort of.

I feel her pain. It sucks. It hurts. And I've been there. It's hard to know how to set your emotional thermostat to what's best for your kid. Do you dive in and fight for them? Take the bull by the horns and go talk some sense into the coach because it feels like they have been slighted? Or do you sit back, bite your tongue, and hope it will all work out for the best?

Here's the deal: because of the ever-growing trend to start playing travel and club sports at younger and younger ages, and because "we don't want our kid to be left out" or "fall behind," this has become an increasingly common issue.

"What are the positives and the negatives of him playing on the second team?" I asked her over the phone.

"Well, he would definitely be one of the stronger players. He'd get a *ton* of playing time and get to be a leader on that team. And while he'd miss all of his closest buddies he'd made over the last two years on the top team, he'd make new friends and grow in ways we probably haven't thought of yet."

"You're right," I said. "I think you have your answer."

When I circled back with her a few weeks later, it was evident she'd handled it beautifully.

"When I told him the news, I just sat with him while he cried," she said. "He had just come home from school, so I redirected the conversation. We discussed several other topics about his day. As the conversation came to a close, I asked him how he was feeling. I intentionally wanted to leave space for him to speak and not be led by my reactions, my reflections, and how I wanted him to process this issue.

"As I listened to how he was processing the situation, it was beautiful to hear him come to some of the same conclusions I had without me 'leading the witness,'" she said. "I realize now that if I had spoken more than I had listened, if I had directed the conversation so he processed it how I wanted him to process it, I would have missed an opportunity to understand my kid better. I would have missed an opportunity to both see how well he *does* deal with challenges and to identify how I can help him in those areas where he is still lacking. I would have missed the opportunity to applaud the best of his resilience and instincts—and be available to help him in the areas where he still needs some guidance."

Wow. I was impressed with how well she'd played the hand the two of them had been dealt. But she wasn't finished.

"It doesn't remove my *desire* to micromanage everything and my wish to control the world around him, particularly when I feel he was wronged. But it allows me to look at my job as understanding and knowing him first. Deciding how to help him is a distant second."

It's the hardest things to do—to let go—but it's often just what the parent-child relationship needs when it comes to sports. A friend of mine told me how, as a young father, he was finding it increasingly difficult to teach his 14-year-old son how to play golf. "He had no patience for the process," the father told me. "I'd offer some instruction and if it didn't work immediately, he'd get frustrated, slam his club down, huff. Finally, on the golf course, my son had a meltdown, with his anger aimed at me."

More out of frustration than design, the father realized this was a turning point. "OK, Reggie," he said. "From now on, let's let it be *your* game—not me trying to teach you *my* game. If you want to play golf with me or want instructions from me, I'll be there for you, night or day. But, meanwhile, it's your game, OK? You lead."

The son was a bit stunned but nodded an OK.

The new setup changed everything. It allowed the son to find his own solutions—and he did. A few years later, he got a job at a local public golf course and, as he was picking up range-ball baskets, began listening to the golf pro give lessons. Gradually, he began implementing the concepts into his own game. At 15, he beat his father for the first time. "I was thrilled!" the dad told me. At 18, his son won the course's club championship, beating a Division I golfer on the first playoff hole. He went on to play competitive golf at a small, private college—and loved it, mainly because of the great friendships he built.

"I'd like to take credit for what he accomplished," the father said, "but the fact is I just got out of the way. At the time, I wasn't thinking: 'Oh, it's important for him to improvise and learn to find solutions on his own, let him put his imagination to work.' But looking back: that's *exactly* what happened. But it couldn't happen until I got out of the way."

I asked the father if the process was hard on his ego. "At first, yeah, but I think he was more willing to include me because

I wasn't *insisting* on it. At age 19, for the state public-course championships, he asked me to caddy for him—and I not only got to just stand back and enjoy watching him play, but I was all the prouder of him because he'd built his game on his own."

What's more, over time, he noticed how the lesson got passed down to another generation. Decades later, the father played a round of golf with his now 41-year-old son and his 15-year-old grandson. "The thing that jumped out at me was that Reggie wasn't at all the 'do-this-do-that' father that I'd been with him. Why? He was letting his son figure it out on his own."

It was all the cooler when, my friend told me, his grandson rolled in a par putt to beat him at the same age, 15, that his son had first beaten him.

"I loved it!" the man told me.

At times, of course, our children need our involvement. At times, it's appropriate to go to a coach with a question—more on that later—and, at times, we might need to do some gentle "butt-kicking" to help our kids understand their commitment to a team. But, in general, look for opportunities to back off. Here are four tips on how to be a "hands-off" parent when necessary.

- **Let your child drive the process.** If he is up at 6 AM, bag packed, itching to get to the soccer field and dying to try out the new move he learned, that's a sign of an internally motivated kid. Kids like that might not make the top team right away but because they love the sport and understand getting better takes work, they will often blossom as stars later.
- **Encourage your child to be curious and ask questions of himself.** "What skills do I need to improve on so I might make the team next year?" "What feedback should I ask Coach for so I can improve my chances going forward?" If he doesn't know the answer, don't panic. That's OK! This is a process. It's a great place to start, which leads to the third step.

- **Encourage your kid set up a one-on-one meeting with the coach.** This will show that he's open to feedback and that he truly wants to get better. This needs to be driven by your child, not *you*. If he is nervous about speaking directly with the coach, you can offer to be there, but tell him, "I'm going to let you do all the talking; let's practice what you'd like to ask." Your child reaching out to the coach will show the coach several key insights: *Here is a kid who really truly wants to get better and isn't just caught up on being on the top team.* And second, *This kid is coachable.* Nine out of ten times coaches will opt for a less-talented athlete who is coachable over one who is ridiculously talented but isn't open to feedback.
- **Support him.** If the issue is him not making a team, ask him how he feels about it. Note: do *not* insert your opinions here. For the moment, swallow your own hurt and sadness, take a deep breath, and ask him what he thinks of his position on his new team. You may be surprised to hear that while he's a bit disappointed, he's actually relieved (less pressure) or excited (different friends he gets to be with). Don't assume it's all bad news.

Dr. Lisa Damour, a psychologist and *New York Times* best-selling author of *Under Pressure* and *Tangled,* encourages parents to refrain from giving unsolicited advice.

"The most powerful force in a normally developing teenager may be the drive toward independence. Unsolicited coaching—even when it is excellent and well-intentioned—goes against the adolescent grain."

As parents, the choice is ours: we can push, push, push—and risk being the parent of a child who, at the basketball banquet, says his most vivid memory is of feeling the scorn of your disapproval. Or we can step back, trust them to find solutions on their own, and watch them go change the world.

Part III

STRATEGY II: RAISING HEALTHY ATHLETES

CHAPTER EIGHT

IS IT WISE TO SPECIALIZE?

Deciding if, and when, to stick with one sport

IF YOU GREW UP in the 1960s, '70s, or '80s and were an athlete, you probably played more than one sport. Jimmy Klein was no exception.

"I played every sport I could get my hands on," said Klein, a 1989 Loyola High (Los Angeles) graduate whose list as a youth included tennis, baseball, soccer, golf, volleyball, football, and basketball. By the time he got to high school, he focused only on football, basketball, and volleyball. And the guy was good. At 6'3", 205 pounds with an explosive 37-inch vertical leap, Klein was big enough to be a defensive back in football but lean enough to play outside hitter in volleyball. Basketball, he told me, was just a "side hustle."

He was an integral part of his high school's state championship football team, which was ranked No. 1 in the country, and made the U.S. Junior Olympics in volleyball. When Klein was a senior, Stanford came calling and said it would allow him to do something rare: play football and volleyball. "I just wanted to take both sports as far as I could," he said.

But that didn't turn out to be very far. Because of the constant stress on his body, his knees gave out. He played one season of volleyball and two of football before he had to give up Division I sports.

He learned the hard way what too many athletes learn only by experience—sometimes there can be too much of a good thing. Pick your cliché, but you get the idea: trying to be great at multiple sports is rarely a wise choice.

Exceptions certainly exist. In the 1990s, former Auburn star Bo Jackson became the only professional athlete in history to be named to an All-Star team in both baseball and football. But it rarely works out well.

Given as much, you might think I'm one of those specialize-from-the-get-go types. Nope. In this chapter, I'll explain why, instead, I favor the "pyramid approach" to youth sports: broad at the base, when the child is young, and narrowing to a point when he or she is approaching the college years.

Sampling versus Specialization

If I had a nickel for every time a parent asked me whether their child should specialize in a particular sport or "play the field," I wouldn't be writing this book; I'd own the publishing company, plus a major share of Google.

Let me be frank. This is a complicated issue and, though I wish it were otherwise, there's no "one-size-fits all" answer. But from my own experience as a Peak Performance Coach, as a parent of athletes, and as a former athlete who in my youth was involved in softball, basketball, tennis, downhill skiing, horseback riding, track & field and, eventually, volleyball, I'm a huge advocate for early sampling.

Benefits abound for kids tasting an array of sports early on. Not only does it lead to greater physical ability and spatial awareness, but it also keeps the "F word"—fun—in the game longer. Why do you think kids in the 1960s and '70s played so much Red Rover and dodgeball in grade school P.E.? Because it was *fun!* (And let's face it, it was probably easy for the P.E. teachers to organize.) Little did those kids know that in doing this they were improving an array of skills from hand-eye coordination to their ability to throw, from team building to learning how to be resilient and communicate with those behind the enemy line with you.

As a parent, among your reasons for involving your kids in sports, I hope, is help them create a lifelong love of physical movement that will keep them healthier and happier into adulthood. Beyond that, you've already read why sports can help grow curious, fun young people into awesome adults. Here, then, are five reasons why letting your child sample an array of different sports before the age of 13 supports that create-great-people goal.

- **It provides kids the opportunity to learn to move their bodies in a variety of ways.** By age 10, Megan loved both ballet and soccer. The core strength she gained from ballet helped her improve her balance and control as a soccer player. And the lateral quickness and foot speed she learned in soccer helped her move gracefully across the floor in a pirouette or grand jete!
- **Diversity of movement—using different muscles—limits the amount of stress and strain on one particular body part.** Maybe you recall the first-chapter story of Jake, the soccer/basketball player who blew out his back. Overuse injuries in swimmers and baseball players (shoulders) are common. If you are repeating the same action over and over, it eventually

leads to the muscle tearing down. By middle-school age, it's now common that pitchers are limited to only a certain number of pitches per day, in order to avoid tearing the medial ulnar collateral ligament (UCL or Tommy John ligament). An arm surgery made famous in 1974 by major league pitcher Tommy John is increasingly common procedure for teens. Nearly 57 percent of all Tommy John surgeries from 2007 to 2011 were performed on 15- to 19-year-olds, according to *The American Journal of Sports Medicine*. This can only be attributed to one thing: overuse.

- **It allows your child interaction in a variety of social settings.** Sports are a great way for kids to learn how to socialize, collaborate, and understand how to work together.

- **It gives your child the opportunity to learn to overcome new challenges by attempting new tasks.** We are creatures of habit and like to do things that we already do well. Learning a new skill allows kids to understand, firsthand, what it means to stick with something even when they might not be the best at it.

- **It offers the joy of being a beginner, which leads to understanding that over their lifetime they can continuously learn new things.** Five-time Olympic volleyball player Danielle Scott-Arruda, at 48, started learning the piano. "Why did you decide to pursue that?" I asked her on my *#RaisingAthletes* podcast. "My eight-year-old is learning to play as well and I thought it would be something fun we could do together. I'm not very good yet, but I don't care. It's really fun to be able to play a duet together." This is the perfect example of a growth mindset. Never stop learning!

OK, not to be a Debbie Downer, but the whole youth-sports scene does have this demarcation point—roughly age 14—where a decision needs to be made. And it's not always "the fun part."

Some high schools encourage kids to play more than one sport their freshmen year as a way to get involved and make more friends. But club programs make it difficult to be able to compete in a high school sport and a club program in more than one sport.

Don't panic. If you have a child who's a "Jimmy kind of kid" who loves more than one sport, here's an idea: have a family meeting with your kid and ask him or her what they want to do. Some kids love the socialization of being on a particular team and aren't bothered about not being a starter; they'd prefer to play on that team, even if it's the only sport in which they're involved. Others might be ready to let go of one sport so they can have the best possible chance of not only making the team but getting as much playing time as possible. Perhaps that's the path you should favor, too.

But don't make the mistake a friend of mine made with his kids: assuming Kid Two has the same passion as Kid One.

"At the time, the assumption came easy for me: both my sons were fairly small for their age and when the oldest hit high school, golf became his thing. He emerged as a great player. So when his younger brother was ready for high school, I assumed he would become an even better golfer than his brother. But at dinner one night he announced he was playing baseball."

My friend was like, "Are you kidding me? You have a sweeter swinger than your brother. Golf's your ticket, kid."

His younger son was a solid baseball player but nothing spectacular; the dad worried that his son would be riding the pines for four years. But he listened to his son's druthers, let him play baseball, and learned that he'd underestimated the kid. He made varsity late in his sophomore year, became a starter as a junior, and made all-league as a senior.

When it comes to how many and which sports your child should play, listen to them instead of forcing your will on them.

"Initially, I thought I knew best," said the father. "Nope, my son knew best."

Or learn from my mistake. I tried to convince my oldest son, CJ, to play two sports his freshman year of high school. I thought it would help increase his vertical and lateral mobility, which I knew he wanted for basketball. I told him, "I don't care if you only play for a year; I think it'll not only be a great way to make some new friends, it'll also help your larger goal of playing basketball in college. It will make you a better athlete."

He had played some volleyball on the middle school team when we lived in New York; I confess, I loved that he tried it—and the bonus was naturally pretty good! Figuring that California boys' volleyball would be even more competitive than in New York, we encouraged him to go out for the high school freshman team. He begrudgingly agreed to try out once basketball was over—because his best friend was trying out. Then came an unexpected twist: *he* made the team, but *his friend* did not.

His reaction stunned my husband and me. He refused to join. He doubled down on the fun teen attitude of "you can't make me do this." Six AM practices were hard enough to drive to when your son *did* want to play, but envisioning dragging him to the gym kicking and screaming wasn't going to be sustainable for me. We relented and allowed him to focus on basketball, which is the only thing he ever wanted to do.

Ah, but the story has an interesting epilogue. The summer after he graduated, as he was reflecting on his high school career, he told me he regretted he hadn't played volleyball.

"It would have been very fun, Mom, even I didn't play all four years."

Ah, the wisdom of hindsight. Parents, I share this story with you because you may be in a similar boat, or just the opposite, and sometimes we need to just let our kids make their own decisions and then live with the outcomes. I'd like to think my encouragement for him to play volleyball has made him more open to new opportunities, like the fact at age 20 he's fallen in love with surfing and really enjoys golf as well. I think it did because he realized he missed out on having fun with a few guys who later in high school became very good friends.

THE FLIP SIDE

Now, before you think my let-'em-play-when-they're-young stance simplifies everything, I need to offer full disclosure. There's also a dark side to going that route. If the situation with your child isn't watched carefully, the experience can turn ugly.

So, three potential downsides for allowing your child to play numerous sports, particularly if starting at ages as young as four:

- **Burnout—both mental and physical.** Taking time off (at least one to two days per week) is critical for these growing athletes. (We'll get into rest and recovery in Chapter 12.)
- **Overuse injuries.** Doing too much, particularly at young ages while their bodies are still growing and muscles, bones, and tendons aren't yet fully developed, can cause irreversible damage in your child. Operative word: *can.* Don't wring your hands because your kid is playing soccer in the fall and basketball in the winter, maybe even baseball in the spring. But *do* keep a close eye on the situation and be cautious about your kid doing too much of the same motion, month after month and year after year.
- **Peaking too early.** There is such a thing as hitting a ceiling in the development of their sport at an earlier age than those who played multiple sports. Coaches will compare a player who is new to a sport but is a great versatile athlete to a player who has only played one sport and see that their raw talent is something they can help mold like clay. "If I have

to choose between a player who has played 10 years of only basketball versus one who has only played three, but has also played lacrosse and run track, I can pretty easily train them."

Considering such concerns regarding burnout, here's how I've seen the one-sport kid focus play out in clients of mine:

- **Mental/physical burnout scenario:** Seth was a strong high school tennis player. At 15, an overuse injury sidelined him for several months. **Outcome:** In his downtime, he started worrying that he'd fallen behind his peers and, once he'd recovered, chose to not return to the courts. He quit tennis altogether. Sad.
- **Overuse injury scenario:** Thomas was a freakishly good athlete from a young age. He was getting DI interest from basketball coaches in the eighth grade. At only 6'1", his windmill dunk was particularly impressive. That is how he played all the time, full out. In addition to going hard on the basketball court almost year-round between high school and club seasons, he was also playing travel baseball. He never took more than a week off per year. **Outcome:** He got a full ride to a DI college, but before his freshman year he suffered a torn ligament in his hip and a sports hernia at the same time, sidelining him for three to five months.
- **Hitting-the-ceiling-early scenario:** John was a nationally rated baseball player. In the eighth grade, he had a verbal offer to play baseball for University of North Carolina. He and his family were so excited by this; his Instagram account was proudly labeled, "UNC Baseball, Class of 2022." But by high school, he had peaked—he wasn't getting better—and UNC rescinded its offer. **Outcome:** He ended up going to another DI program, but he wasn't offered a scholarship.

Whether because of injury, burnout, or peaking too soon, sports specialization can narrow your child's future opportunities.

It's tough to predict how much is too much because each kid is different, and each person's body and tolerance is different. But, generally speaking, think like the financial advisor who says, "It is wise to diversify." Putting all your eggs in one basket can limit, not expand, your child's opportunities down the road.

A few questions to ask about your children in guiding you to a decision:

- Are they getting something out of each sport they are playing?
- Are they happy about doing multiple activities?
- Are they still getting rest and downtime or does their schedule dictate every waking minute of their day? They need a day or two off each week to recover—mentally and physically. Talk to them. See how they're doing with things.

"Isabella, I noticed that between soccer and lacrosse, in addition to your academic load, you're burning the candle at both ends. How are you feeling about it?"

Your children only get one shot at childhood, and you want them to look back with fond memories of the teams they played on and the friends they made. You don't want them to remember it as a pressure-packed haze of rushing here and there.

One mother's story has always stuck with me. "When my older son was graduating from high school, I asked him if he was going to miss soccer," she told me. "He smiled sweetly at me and said, 'Oh, Mom, I stopped enjoying playing soccer many years ago. But I could tell how important it was to you. That's the only reason I kept playing.'"

It stopped her dead in her tracks. "You mean I could have avoided all of those weekend road trips, sitting on the sidelines in the freezing New York rain and late nights—if I'd only asked you sooner?"

CHAPTER NINE

HARDCORE COMPETITORS AT AGE FIVE

*Assessing the timing and opportunity
of competitive versus rec ball*

SCOTT SCHULTZ WAS THE COOLEST, calmest dad in the bleachers at the third-grade basketball game that sunny morning in Encinitas, California. All the other parents were losing their minds every time the pack of nine-year-old boys followed the ball up and down the floor, with the ball only occasionally getting anywhere near one of the rims. He was so nonchalant, in fact, that, as a youth sports junky, I couldn't help myself.

"He must not be your oldest child," I said. "You're *way* too calm."

His Cheshire grin said it all, but over the course of the next several missed baskets, he told me his story anyway. In fact, Charlie was his fifth child. He said he'd watched more youth sports in the last 20 years than he'd ever imagined possible.

"Believe me, I used to *not* be this calm. I've learned a lot raising five children. Probably the biggest and most painful lesson I learned was from the mistakes we made with our oldest son, Tim."

Little Timmy Shultz was a natural on the golf course. Scott remembers taking him to the driving range and being amazed by how much patience, focus, and serenity he exuded even as a young ankle-biter at age five. "His golf bag was bigger than he was. He could barely carry it. He was so drawn to the sport, he would gladly stand there for hours hitting balls. And much to my surprise, he was open to my coaching, so he quickly got better. I love golf, so what started off as 'daddy and me' time at the driving range quickly evolved by age six or seven into enrolling him in California Junior Golf and eventually American Junior Golf tournaments every weekend."

Despite having four other kids, a time-consuming job, and little free time when Timmy started playing competitively at six, Scott reflects on how enamored he and his wife, Christie, were by what they heard from pros at every course Timmy played.

"'Wow, your son has a lot of talent. Check out that natural swing. Look out, Tiger Woods!' they'd say. We were excited about his growing love of the game and how quickly his handicap was plummeting. Christie and I could picture, probably all too clearly, a life of watching him one day play, if not on the tour, at least, in college."

The more they watched, the deeper the involvement got. "Once you are traveling to all of the junior tournaments, you meet hundreds of other parents just like you. We got completely caught up in the madness of it. All of the family's free time and vacations ended up revolving around Timmy's golf. His younger siblings spent more free time at golf tournaments than they did playing in our neighborhood with friends. When I look back on it now, I realize it was a fun time, but it gives me pause. I definitely parent Charlie differently than I did Tim."

Over time, Tim grew into a highly competitive golfer, so much so that when he was in high school Stanford came calling. His folks had hit the proverbial sports-parenting lottery! Stanford offered him a full-ride scholarship and a chance to play with the best collegiate golfers in the country.

Suddenly, as he was telling this story beyond the clamor of the gym, Scott's voice softened. Tim's journey took a sudden turn.

"He had accepted the scholarship to Stanford. We were thrilled to send him off on what we thought was his dream, to play golf in college. But less than a month before he was supposed to go, he came to my wife and I and said, 'I can't go.' We assumed he was injured or scared of leaving home but were not prepared for what came next. 'I don't love golf,' he said. 'In fact, I haven't even *liked* it for a long time. I just got so good and I knew it made you both proud, I couldn't quit. But I can't go to Stanford. I don't want to play anymore. And I don't want to go to school there.'"

I had to pick my jaw up off the bleacher seats. So, this was why he cheered so casually for his child! "If he loves it, great; if not, that's OK, too," Scott said about his fifth child, Charlie.

"So," I said, "did Tim wind up going to college?"

"Yes, San Jose State University. He seems happy with it. But he hasn't picked up a set of clubs since he made the decision."

Parents, this is such a heartbreaking story because it can become your worst fear realized. If you have a child who excels early and seems to love it, what parent wouldn't move mountains to help them get better? I hear from a lot from parents who are in the middle of raising their child and insist, "Well, it's all her. It has been since she was three."

Really? Are you sure she demanded going out and hitting tennis balls every day of the week? Even if she did, what did you do to help her find perspective along the way? That's what we're all striving for here. Helping our kids discover their passions while finding perspective in life even during the middle of the excitement of them growing into bigger, stronger, better athletes.

What's Driving Your Athlete?

Meet Raquel, a Division I volleyball player and a former neighbor. She played multiple sports until she found her calling with volleyball at 13. Despite being nearly 6'0" tall, she had come "late to the game" by today's youth sports standards, so she didn't make her middle school team. But she gratefully took on the role of manager that season, which allowed her to practice and to get more reps. She also quickly realized she needed to join a volleyball club so she could accelerate her development. Her parents, let's call them Doug and Tammy, were very supportive of her pursuing volleyball and eagerly agreed to sign her up to play club.

Doug says has no regrets for how Raquel's volleyball career has turned out. Despite spending thousands of dollars on club fees, travel costs, and hotels for tournaments, private coaching, even hiring a college recruiting coach who helped Raquel get a "mix tape" together and blast it out to over a hundred DI schools, he believes it was all worth it. That being said—and with hindsight being 20/20, now that he's on the other side of his daughter's quest to get a college scholarship—he's got some wisdom to share with parents about the process. "What gets lost in [the youth sports process] is the kid themselves. No one stops to ask them what they want," he said.

"I was the dad who, when Raquel was in eighth grade, was *all* in. I was worried about which club level volleyball team she was on. I thought it was so important that she played on the

1's team. She started on the 3's team and worked her way up. By the time she was a sophomore, she'd made the top team and all of the parents on that team, me included, were chasing scholarships. Looking back now, it isn't what I expected it was going to be," he quietly reflected.

When I asked him what he thought he was getting into back then and what advice he has for parents who are on the front end of deciding whether their child should play club or not, he paused, sighed, and finally uttered, "I don't know. But it wasn't that. I thought I was just doing what was best for my child. I think the parents are sometimes ruining [sports] for their kids.

"The process is chaotic. There is a lot of pressure to get recruited when you're playing for the top team. Sometimes I wonder if we would have ever even considered hiring a recruiting coordinator or sending out hundreds of emails if she wasn't surrounded by others who were doing the same."

Raquel says her love of volleyball kept growing each year she played until she first hit a headwind her senior year. "I loved my high school team; it was so fun! But the club competitions were so serious. There was so much pressure to win and be ranked. That took over. I spent my entire senior year of club dreading it and saying, 'I can't wait for this to be over.'"

Parents, perhaps you have an athlete who loves her sport but you can't tell if it's something she really wants to commit to playing for another four years. Perhaps she's just like Raquel and is just surrounded by others (athletes and parents) who do. Perhaps she has gotten really good at her sport so is hearing from college coaches that she could play. That makes her curious about whether it's possible or not.

It's a big decision and one that shouldn't be taken lightly. Sometimes the joy and passion you've watched grow in your child as she's developed while playing has run its course and the time has come to pivot onto the next phase of life. But the big question for parents is, how do you know? I'll get to that but first let's talk about other factors that are also causing kids to quit playing sports.

COVID-19 played a major role in kids deciding they are done playing sports. Recently the Aspen Institute, an organization that studies sports as well as other important subjects, issued its State of Play 2020 report ("Youth Sports take a Punch from the Pandemic," *Washington Post*, October 21, 2020). A thousand kids ages six to 18 were interviewed. One part of the report examined the effects of the pandemic on kids' sports and how kids play. The study uncovered that 29 percent of kids say they are no longer interested in playing sports. These aren't kids who sat on the couch all day; they're kids who used to play sports before the pandemic.

Whether it's a shift from their level of interest and intensity prior to COVID or you sense they may have a reticence to continue playing to the next level, be it high school or college, here are a few talking points to get the conversation going with your teen. This should be a mostly one-way dialog between you and your teen. They should be doing most of the talking. Head nods and listening intently to understand where they are coming from in their point of view are welcome from you. Try to avoid jumping in to give them the answer. This is their journey and they need to come to the decision (with your help).

- **Ask him *why* he started playing.** Whether it was a fun memory of how he used to practice in his own in the backyard until dark or from a time when he was younger and he had a wonderful game that you can both still recall with fondness.

- ***What* is it about this sport that she continues to enjoy most?** Some love tennis because there is no one else to count on: "It's just me out there and either I play well and win or I stink it up and I lose." Others love softball because of the team element. "I love being with the other girls, we have so much fun together in the dugout. They are my best friends."

- **What other activities do you find interesting?** I have one client who took up running with her dog, "I never used to find it all that exciting, but when COVID hit and I couldn't participate in soccer or volleyball, running with my dog, Stormie, became my dream time," 12-year-old Lila told me. "Fresh air and alone time felt great."

- **If she were to pivot away from the sport that she's been playing up to this point, what would she do in place of all the time that would then become available?** A different sport? Cooking? Drawing? Volunteering?

As I'll discuss about in more depth in Chapter 16, "Push Through or Pivot," there will come a time for every athlete when she will have to say good-bye to competition. Even the world's best athletes have an expiration date on their competitive careers. Having your athlete check in regularly with themselves at each stage along their sports journey and answer whether they want to continue pursuing this particular sport is a critical step for long-term success.

Doug admits that now that Raquel is playing DI volleyball, and it's a full-time job for her. She probably missed out on a lot of fun in high school because every free moment was taken trying to help her get better. "We didn't want to miss an opportunity. Raquel was definitely on board and would agree that it was her choice to play college volleyball, but the journey was anything but straight forward or stress free. If she had a day off, instead of encouraging her to go to the beach and hang with friends, we'd suggest she better get to the gym and get a private lesson. She was happy to go along with it; it wasn't us forcing an agenda, but I kind of regret it."

Doug shared some more wisdom for parents, "What I didn't realize back then was what was most important in order for Raquel to get better was that she needed to be on the court playing during the tournaments and the level didn't really matter, particularly at the younger ages. Also, Raquel only played as a right-side hitter so she never learned how to pass the ball or play another position. My biggest advice to parents of young athletes is twofold: have them play more than one sport and within a given sport, play as many positions as possible."

There are a lot of factors you ultimately don't have control over—how tall your child will eventually become or what each team's needs will be. But if your daughter has skills that allow her to play multiple positions, she'll get more playing time and more playing time will help her grow both physically and mentally. Ultimately, if she gains confidence, leadership skills and understand her strengths and weaknesses better, you've succeeded as a parent."

Raquel proudly agrees: "Yes, I know that my athletic journey, while not perfect, will help me with whatever I choose to do next in life. I'm excited about the future and grateful for what playing sports has taught me."

Parents, there is no "one size fits all" approach for raising an athlete. But what I hope you'll consider along the way is what feels right for you and your family and most importantly what feels right for your child. This has to be an intrinsically driven process. If it's being forced upon them too early or for too long, it won't be sustainable. Just ask seven-time Super Bowl champion, Tom Brady, if he'll retire. "I'll retire when I'm no longer having fun or don't think I can get any better. Luckily for me, that hasn't happened yet."

CHAPTER TEN

HOW TO LIMIT ATHLETIC POTENTIAL

Why nutrition, sleep, and downtime matter so much

IN 2019 I WAS INVITED TO SPEAK to parents of student-athletes at Marlborough, a private all-girls school in Los Angeles, about the challenges of raising athletes and how to help them balance the pressures student athletes are under. As parents, we're always trying to figure out how to keep all our kids' plates spinning, among them academics, competitive sports, volunteering, social-justice causes, student council—you get the idea. In addition, of course, to finding time to unwind, relax and—oh, right—be a teenager.

After the talk, as I chatted with a handful of parents, I was stunned by one father's story. He was justifiably proud of a daughter who was a sophomore at an Ivy League school. In addition to being pre-med, she was an all-league pole vaulter on the track team.

"She must be very disciplined and manage her time well," I said.

"She got used to not getting a lot of sleep during high school."

"Meaning?"

"After all the homework she had to do, she routinely got only four to five hours of sleep a night. That's all she had time for. She took three or four Advanced Placement classes her junior and senior years, was part of the student council, and was studying for the ACT—on top of competing in track, of course."

"Excuse me," I said. "Are you suggesting she never slept more than five hours a night?"

"That's right," he said with a worrisome hint of pride. "She lived on Red Bull and adrenaline."

"And how she's doing now?"

"College has been very challenging—pre-med and track. She still doesn't sleep much. It's looking like she may need to drop track. May not be sustainable to keep doing both well—and stay healthy."

The smarmy side of me wanted to say, "Ya think?" The more compassionate side hoped her years of sleep-deprivation wouldn't come back to haunt her. And the author side sent an ASAP message to my brain: *Gotta have a chapter about young athletes not letting their involvement in sports steal their health.*

"If you want to set your teen up for a collision course with disaster, deprive them of healthy food, restrict their sleep, and give them little to no time off," said Dr. Dolly Klock, a family physician in Los Angeles.

She is founder of Adolessons, a company that helps parents and their t(w)eens understand the changes kids' bodies go through as they approach puberty—and get beyond it. The two of us have partnered multiple times on talks to parents. She focuses on the physical and emotional changes of puberty, and I speak on peak performance opportunities our kids have when they take care of their bodies. The two of us intersect at three important points: sleep, rest, and nutrition.

We can, Dolly says, get away with cutting the corners on a short-term basis—months, perhaps even a few years. But year after year? The person is a walking time bomb.

Recently my next-door neighbor apologized to me for the rickety old car that had been parked in front of their house for months on end—undriven. "My daughter didn't think much of the 'check engine' light that had been on for months, until she ran out of oil and the car stopped on the side of the 405 freeway," said her father, a tad annoyed.

Parents, our job is to help our kids learn how to manage their schedules in moderation, fuel their systems in a healthy but not overly restrictive way—hey, they're teenagers!—and, most importantly, get the sleep their growing bodies need!

Before our kid's check-engine light flashes on, let's look at nutrition, sleep, and rest:

NUTRITION

When my oldest son, CJ, was 12, he spent the night at his sixth-grade friend Joe's house.

"How'd it go?" I asked the next morning.

He mentioned staying up all night watching *The Dark Knight* on repeat, eating cheese pizza, and drinking pop. But the bigger takeaway was seeing Joe's older college-age brother, Drew.

"Mom, Drew walks shirtless at eight in the morning, flexing his muscles, drinking his protein shakes and teasing Joe and I how small and skinny we are," said the 98-pound weakling. "It's so funny. All he cares about is his body."

I just smiled. "Is that so?"

Five years later, my husband and I traded knowing glances after the former rail-thin pizza wimp strolled in after a workout with no shirt, casually slapping his abs.

"We got any protein shakes?"

Sometimes, if we're lucky, our kids will begin to understand the cause-and-effect of nutrition on their own: eat well, compete better, feel better, look better. Other times, they might need a nudge.

Give them plenty of options—beyond processed foods such as french fries, potato chips, candy, and soda. Figure out what whole foods your teenager likes and will be good for him, the kind of stuff that ten-time Super Bowl quarterback Tom Brady eats. A sampling: avocado and eggs for breakfast; salads with nuts and fish for lunch; hummus, guacamole, or mixed nuts for snacks; roasted vegetables and chicken for dinner; and berry or banana smoothies before workouts. Other go-to snacks that work: grapes, blueberries, apples, pears, bananas, and veggies like cucumbers, kale, and spinach.

Some people are able to eat junk food and not suffer weight gain, but weight isn't the only problem with bad food. It makes your child more susceptible to injury. Derek Cox, a former NFL player and client of mine, told me it wasn't until a nutritionist came to speak to his NFL team, the Jacksonville Jaguars, that he understood how important good nutrition was. He completely changed his diet, replacing bad food with good food—and was stunned at the difference. In fact, when I met him for lunch at a cafe in Santa Monica, after he was five years out of the league, I was surprised how "clean" he ate. He asked the waitress to remove the corn; "too much sugar."

And while he's taking the corn out of his salad, I casually asked, "So I guess this means you don't drink coffee or alcohol, much less eat sugar, then?"

You would have thought I'd asked him to drink cyanide. "Nope, don't touch any of that poison. It really sabotages your performance."

"But you're not even playing professionally anymore," I added.

"Nope, I got rid of all of that and never looked back." Wow. I'm impressed.

"The average player lasts three years in the league," he said. "I made it seven years and I 100 percent attribute that longevity to the whole-food diet I adopted. I never missed a game due to injury. It was a complete game-changer for me."

When helping your kid transition to a better diet, allow her to sample different foods. Even if she isn't a super healthy eater, she may find some good, and likable, options.

When my children were young and my husband travelled a lot, I heard some wonderful advice from a family psychologist. "It isn't necessary to have every single member of the family at the dinner table every night. Family dinner is about taking the time for everyone *who is available* to gather."

So, don't feel guilty if it's impossible to always eat together. On the other hand, appreciate the value when you do. "Half of the purpose is about the healthy food you are consuming together." the doctor said. "The other half is about connection. This is your child(ren)'s time to connect with you and each other and speak about the high and low points of their day."

Ironically, one of the silver linings of COVID-19 was the increase in family dinner time, both frequency and duration. If you feel you have nothing "exciting" to talk about, buy some trivia cards to pass around as you eat. They make great conversation starters and it's a wonderful way for each person to feel seen and heard—while, of course, they're eating healthy food.

Sleep

Beyond nutrition, consistently getting ample sleep is important for our children's growing brains and bodies. Adolescents who don't get enough sleep have a higher risk for many health problems. The American Academy of Sleep recommends six-to-12-year-olds get nine to 12 hours of sleep per 24-hour period and 13-to-18-year-olds get eight to 10 hours.

As my opening story about the "five-hour-wonder" suggests, it's possible for our children to operate from a "sleep deficit" and survive for extended periods of time. But what if they didn't have a deficit? How much better might they be—in sports *and* academics? Studies show that athletes are more effective when they get adequate sleep.

A study done with the Stanford men's basketball teams between 2005 and 2008 measured sleep extension to see if it was beneficial to athletic performance, reaction time, vigor, fatigue, and mood in collegiate basketball players. The short answer: yup! The same players who reported seven or fewer hours of sleep per night showed marked statistical shooting improvement when they got an average of 8.5 hours. With increased sleep they improved on free throw accuracy (7.9 makes out of 10 attempts to 8.8) and on three-point accuracy (10.2 makes out of 15 attempts to 11.6). Not only did shot percentage improve, but reaction times increased, daytime sleepiness decreased, and their general moods improved.

I can already hear some of you: "Yeah, great, but how do you get a teenager to get to bed on time?"

Back to Dr. Klock: "As teens hit puberty, their circadian rhythms shift, which is why they naturally want to go to bed later and sleep later. But the later they stay up doing homework, the more inefficient they become. This also is what causes the sleep deficit and the whole thing compounds the following day."

A few tips related to sleep for peak performance (for teens and adults alike) based on the findings from the Stanford sleep study:

- Prioritize sleep as a part of your regular training regimen.
- Extend nightly sleep for several weeks to reduce your sleep debt before competition.

- Maintain a low sleep debt by obtaining a sufficient amount of nightly sleep (seven to nine hours for adults, nine or more hours for teens and young adults).
- Keep a regular sleep-wake schedule, going to bed and waking up at the same times every day.
- Take brief 20–30 minute naps to obtain additional sleep during the day, especially if drowsy.

Rest & Recovery

Walk onto any field, into any gym, or onto any pool deck in America where teens are competing and, over time, you'll hear the too-much-of-a-good-thing stories. Kids who overdid it and got hurt because of it. Overwork that led to chronic knee, back, or shoulder injuries.

The degree of overuse injuries for young athletes is at unprecedented levels. With the decrease in teens playing multiple sports and the increase in them playing a single sport year-round, the pounding that the young, growing bodies undergo is asking a price. Unfortunately, that sometime means permanent injuries.

Nia came from a family of talented athletes. Her grandfather played in the NFL. Her dad, four cousins, and an aunt and uncle were DI and pro athletes as well, so it was not surprising that when she took up volleyball at 10 years old, she was good. A natural, she played other sports like basketball and soccer early on but by 12 quit other sports to focus on volleyball. As a "setter," she was playing up a level in club sports and getting stronger every year; her dream of playing in college was starting to look reachable.

But as a setter, which is to volleyball what quarterbacks are to football, she was active on nearly every play. Lots of pressure on her mind, lots of pressure on her body.

No one saw it coming. But the constant and repetitive strain on her lower back eventually took its toll. Early in her sophomore year she started having lower-back pain. She would rest by taking a few days off, only to come back to practice and have the pain return. Physical therapy didn't help, so she rested for six months. But even that didn't work. Finally, she went to her parents.

"I'm going to change positions. Despite never having been a passer, I feel like the best opportunity for me to get to play the game I love is to give up the position that's causing me pain."

Wow. That took courage. But it allowed her to keep playing.

Look, sports isn't science. We can't measure why and how things happen as they do—and know exactly why, for example, Nia's body broke down when others did not. Likewise, we can't predict the future—whether Nia's back problems will allow her to keep playing. But here's a general truth: if your child is playing a club sport half the year and a middle school or high school sport the other half of the year, she will be afforded little rest. And that's dangerous.

My advice to Nia's parents was to let her embrace this new role. As hard as it may be for the parents, look at it through her eyes: she's a beginner at this position, yes, but it's a new challenge.

"She's a smart, ambitious girl," I said. "This can become a story of success; it doesn't have to spell doom. Change can be good."

In some ways, I could relate to her. A volleyball player, I injured my shoulder my redshirt sophomore year of college. I am left-handed (which is a huge advantage because you can attack the ball when it's close to the net) and 5'11", so the coach said: "You'd make a good setter." Wanting desperately to continue playing, I pivoted. I always said I didn't have the best hands in the game, but my leadership skills, height, and hitting and blocking ability made up for my lack of "soft hands."

Parents, in a few words: give your kids a break. And I don't offer that as a smarmy comment; I mean *literally* give your kids a break. Some tips in that regard:

- Find opportunities to allow them rest. If you know a long weekend is coming up and you are seeing them struggling with fatigue, help them by prioritizing family and down time with, and for, them. They don't want to disappoint you, but if you give them the permission, their bodies (and minds) will thank you later.
- They need one or two days off per week. While this sounds like it would be easy to manage, most teams have conditioning on the days they aren't on the court/field. Help them find time to unwind and recover. Have a family discussion and let them decide where and when it's best for them to take breaks. Blake Mycoskie, multi-millionaire founder of Toms Shoes, says, "As an entrepreneur you really can't afford to take any breaks; there is always something you can be doing to move the business forward. So, I block out one-on-one time with each of my kids. If I didn't do it, it wouldn't happen." Likewise, block out down time for your kids; otherwise, it might not happen.
- Help them find hobbies and "give-back" opportunities to fill the void. Help them fill down time normally dedicated to sports with something that benefits someone else: referee a youth sports league; coach a younger sibling (maybe even make a little money!); volunteer for something that's meaningful to them—whatever allows them to see that gratitude is the key to appreciating what they have.

Finally, remember: they will remember only half of what we *tell them* but almost all of what they *see*. So, as a parent, model as much of the healthy behavior as you can. Get your sleep, eat well, and take time to relax. Not only will this encourage them to do the same, but it will show them how "adulting" works.

After all, we're not only trying to create great kids right now, but great adults for the future!

CHAPTER ELEVEN

THE MINDSET TOOLBOX

*The importance of building resilience
versus avoiding burnout*

"Hi, Kirsten."

The text came in late the night before I was supposed to meet with a longstanding, twice-weekly tennis client, Aaliyah, age 14.

It was her mom, Cherie.

> I am afraid to report that Aaliyah has taken a deep dive back into the dark side. It has been a very tough month of behavior, negativity, and severe victim mentality. I am sending her to stay with my parents for a few days to take a break and hopefully get some perspective.
>
> All I can assume is that she must be feeling so much insecurity and chaos inside herself to be reacting and treating all of us in the way she is. However, no matter how sincerely we try to address this, she gets extremely defensive and spits venom at all of us.

I am not really sure where to go from here. She is not being honest with herself or in her conversations with you, which is why there is a complete block to accepting information that can help her.

I will reach back out after she gets home. I love and believe in the work you do with her—but not when she is unwilling to accept it.

This one blew me away. The previous several months she had been on a slow but mostly increasingly steady mental climb out of an inconsistent pattern of on-court play. She played extremely well against opponents three or four years older than her but imploded when playing girls her own age group who were ranked far lower than she was.

"I feel like the older players are easier for me to compete against," Aaliyah had told me. "When I realize I'm several years younger and lower ranked than an opponent, it takes all the pressure off me mentally and I can perform and play my best."

It was a different story with opponents similar in age. "I sense that the opponent knows she can just get me mad and I'll self-destruct, so she just makes one or two 'cheating' calls like calling a ball that is clearly in, out."

At the junior tennis level, there are no line judges, so players are required to make their own line calls and being truthful isn't always the case. Aaliyah confessed that when another girl was obviously cheating, she felt no other choice but to make a few bad calls as well to "level the playing field." But when that happened, she felt her internal thermometer go from a balmy 65 to center-of-the-sun hot.

In the previous several months, we had been discussing what she felt was holding her back. She admitted her fiery temper was an issue. "And then there's my mom. I know she loves me and supports me, but our relationship usually heads south the day before any big competition."

On one group call, the three of us were chatting about such dynamics when Cherie, the mother, admitted as much. The day before any big event, they both ended up shouting and crying on the long drive home through LA traffic.

"Why do you think that is?" I asked them both.

Said Mom: "There are things Aaliyah has been working on all week with her trainer, things we've identified as areas for improvement, and for some reason the day before she's going to play a big tourney, she just forgets all of it and I spend the entire practice reminding her."

"And how does that work for you, Aaliyah? Your mom giving reminders while you're on the court?"

"Honestly, it's very annoying. I'm not trying to forget everything we worked on, it just sometimes happens. When she interrupts me after every swing, it becomes overwhelming, and things quickly unravel."

We discussed a plan, which they both agreed upon, where Mom wouldn't say anything during the practice. If Aaliyah needed help remembering, Mom could write things down and then at 20- or 30-minute intervals, during a water break, share a thing or two she thought Aaliyah needed to hear. Both agreed that was a good plan.

So, I was shocked to receive the text above a few days later. Clearly, the improvement I was hoping for in their relationship wasn't happening. People, I was reminded, aren't robots. You can't just program them and, shabam, the problems go away. My guess is each of them took a step in the right direction; the new system might have even worked that day. But as stress set in and fear grew, they reverted to their comfort zones. As human beings, that's our tendency; to find our safe place, even if it means being angry with someone else. Even if we know it's not the most productive way to operate, it makes us feel better because it's *what we know.*

But there's a better way, and to find that way you need to understand what I call "mindset tools."

This is our longest chapter, but if you read only one chapter of this book, I believe this should be it. It's the one that could have the most lasting impact for both you and your athlete, provided you not only learn these lessons but implement them in your daily life.

Mindset tools are like going to the gym. You don't get stronger by thinking about lifting weights; you have to do the reps. These tools aren't only for athletes; parents, they are good for you, too. And you shouldn't use them only for sports or only during stressful situations. In fact, most successful people use such tools as part of their daily rituals.

There are two parts to understand: first, *what* tools you need to improve your mental outlook and become grittier. Second, *how* to implement them. Let's start with what I like to call the five C's of growing grit:

No. 1: Clarity

What's the goal? Are you trying to make the varsity team or is your aim higher, to, say, play in college one day? It's about getting clear on what Steven Kotler, in his book *The Art of Impossible, A Peak Performance Primer,* calls High Hard Goals (HHG).

High hard goals are ones that aren't impossible to accomplish, they're just something you've never done before. You know it is attainable, you've watched others do it. It's just not something *you* have achieved yet.

For example, up until the early 1950s, no man had ever run a mile in under four minutes. Most said, "It's not possible," because it hadn't been done. But on May 6, 1954, British runner Roger Bannister ran the first four-minute mile (3:59.4). Within weeks, someone else did it as well. To date, 1,663 athletes have broken the sub-four-minute mile. In the 68 years since Bannister's famous race, the mile record has been lowered by almost 17 seconds, currently standing at 3:43.13, by Hicham El Guerrouj of Morocco. It's impossible, until someone does it.

So what high hard goals are you working toward?

Tips for Good Goal Setting

Be as specific as possible. Write it down as if it's already happened. Your brain doesn't know the difference between you *thinking* something has happened and it having actually happened, so write it down as if it already has. Details matter when creating your future. If you say, "I'd like to be wealthy one day," that's too general. One person's definition of wealth and timing is entirely different than the next person's. Instead, write, "It feels so good to have attained my monthly income goal of netting XX dollars per month." Writing *SMART* goals (specific, measurable, achievable, realistic, and time-bound) means writing good goals. And they should be things within your power, i.e., you may want to win the state championship in soccer, but you alone don't have control over that outcome. What you do have control over is how hard you work out, how often you work out, how focused you are during your workouts, etc. Choose daily goals that align with your High Hard Goals.

Write three HHG below. If you're a parent working with your athlete, ask them to list what they hope to accomplish in the next year:

HHG No. 1)

HHG No. 2)

HHG No. 3)

Now, for each of those goals, write one to three things you could do make that goal become a reality. For example, if HHG No. 1 is to play college soccer:

- "Work on my footwork and agility by coming to practice 30 minutes early each time."
- "Become a more vocal player so I can be seen as a leader by increasing my energy every practice and connecting with my teammates."
- "Keep on top of my academics and get the best grades I can so I can put myself in the position to be recruited by the schools I'd like to attend."

HHG No.1:
Daily goal No. 1)
Daily goal No. 2)
Daily goal No. 3)

No. 2: (Self) Care

We're hardwired to focus on threats and fear. When we spend all our time on a social media diet heavy on current events, we lock in that fear. On social media, have you ever noticed that if you "like" a picture of a cute puppy, you get more cute puppies popping up in your feed? Well, it's the same for whatever we are feeding our subconscious brain.

What do you desire to have more of? Peace, tranquility, and calm, yet you're making choices that only attract more fear.

Exercise: do a one-day audit of where you're spending your "free time."

Do you ever find you are you "doom scrolling"? You mindlessly decide to check out Instagram, Facebook, Snapchat, or TikTok and the next thing you know you have spent countless hours seeing that Katarina's Greek vacation on the 70' yacht was way cooler than your camping trip in grandma's back yard. And now how do you feel? Not only uncool but unmotivated and not interested in even trying to keep up. *Ugh.*

If you've got some HHGs, then what others are doing or who they are doing it with should be of little concern to you. If you find it doesn't bother you to look at others' social media feeds and their "perfect" stress-free lives, then have at it—in limited quantities. But if you find that it just makes you feel "less than" or even worse, depressed, unplug. Now!

Find things that help you recharge:

- Napping
- Journaling
- Reading
- Connecting with a friend or family member
- Playing an instrument, gardening, baking, etc.
- Meditating
- Taking care of small (mindless) tasks

Sometimes when I don't feel up to working on my next presentation, I'll pay a few bills or update my calendar with the kids' schedules. Sometimes doing the little things helps you feel better about the moment that can lead to tackling a bigger project.

No. 3: Contribution

How are your kids paying it forward? One of the best pieces of advice I've heard and now share is when you're not feeling good about yourself, give to others. It's easy to compare yourself to others and think you're not as well off, but when you get outside your personal wants and needs and put someone else's in front of you, your perspective will change for the better.

Midway through COVID, when people were starting to get back outside a bit, I ran into my neighbor, Lisa, walking out her front door. They have one son, Jordan, who was eight years old at the time and obsessed with basketball. So much so, that Parker would often see him peeking his little button nose through the fence to watch Parker shoot. I was telling her how sweet that was and suggested he should come over and shoot with Parker. "Really? B-I-G Parker would be willing to shoot with Jordan?"

"Of course he could!"

So Sunday afternoons for several months, Jordan would come over into the driveway and I'd sneak a peek to find them stretching together to warm up, or working on "fingertip, wrinkle wrist, cookie jar," or practicing layups on the 8' hoop. Parker was super animated with him, and Jordan loved it, "You're the man, J! You're going to be dunking soon!"

It made Parker smile. He remembered being exactly that age and getting to go to NBA MVP Kawhi Leonard's basketball camp. We have a photo of him with Kawhi, who is bending at the waist just to get his head in the photo. So sweet. When you can, take the opportunity to give back; you will get more out of it than the person on the receiving end. I promise. In fact, your body produces a hormone called oxytocin. It is secreted from the pituitary glands in joyous moments. You know how good it feels to hug your spouse or child? Or to play with your dog? That is oxytocin. It lowers the stress hormone cortisol and allows us to relax and find joy in life's simple pleasures, like shooting hoops in the driveway.

No. 4: CREATE

In 2008 the U.S. economy collapsed. While most people were "playing it safe" and just trying to avoid getting laid off or losing their home, others were doubling down on new ideas. Venmo, Uber, Groupon, Slack, Pinterest, and Instagram—all were founded during the 2008–2010 window. It would have been understandable for companies to *not* take risks and to *not* invest in ideas that were untested in a down market. But as Warren Buffet famously said about such investing strategies, "We simply attempt to be fearful when others are greedy and to be greedy only when others are fearful."

So, what are *you* feeling creative about enough to be risky? Even when you're fearful? Even when you can't see how your adventure will play out? It's easy to bet on yourself when you've already had proven success. But what about when it's still a dream? When it's something you'd love to accomplish but you just can't fathom how you'd get from your current state to that finish line? For example, what about trying to make the varsity team as a freshman? Why not?

Of course, the answer is never as simple as wishing or hoping or thinking it into being. But there are some things you do have total control over that can help you get clarity on what you are creating and why you're creating it, which will lead to a plethora of "how" steps.

Daily Tools for Peak Performance

This is the secret sauce. If you're looking for *one* answer to all of your questions, look no further; you've found it. Wouldn't that be great? The ability to just snap your fingers and get whatever you want.

Well, the answer isn't quite that easy, but it is that simple. The answer is having a morning ritual. When I ask teen clients what their morning routines are, chief among them is hitting the snooze as many times as possible. Only when it looks as if the bus or carpool will be missed do some kids spring into action. The side effect might be a missed breakfast, or homework or lunch left on the kitchen table, which leads to more negative outcomes.

There's a better way.

Establishing a Mindfulness or Meditation Practice

Some people pray, while others meditate, but the goal is to have 10–20 minutes first thing in the morning before your day gets started. Sit in a space away from your bed with your back straight and head free. Your eyes can be closed or you can soften your gaze—look to the floor or an object.

Take a few deep breaths in through your nose and out through your mouth. Allow your body to settle and your mind to relax. Imagine there are clouds floating in the sky above you. If those clouds were words or ideas, your goal is to observe them floating by.

Don't judge them. Don't try and solve anything. Just be an observer. One of the biggest misconceptions about meditation is that you should eliminate all thought. That's like asking your heart to stop beating. The word *meditate* means "to think or reflect upon, consider, design, purpose, intend."

Listen to what's going on around you. Do you hear the bird chirping? Or the train going by? Perhaps the noise of the air conditioner is making a buzz. Try and be aware of the sounds, the temperature, the environment. If you feel like you are getting "monkey mind," and all you can think about is your day's "to-dos," this exercise is essential.

Box Breaths

One exercise is deep breath in through the nose, count to five
1.2.3.4.5...
Hold your breath and count to five
1.2.3.4.5...
Breathe out through your mouth for five counts
1.2.3.4.5...
Hold for five counts.

Repeat this at least two or three times. You can build up as you grow accustomed to this routine.

An array of meditation techniques and strategies exist. But if you have never practiced meditation before, start with a mindfulness app like Calm or Headspace. While this isn't meditation—the apps offer words—it does help calm the mind and relax the limbic system.

Mantras: "Things Are Always Working Out for Me."
What are the sayings you have running through your mind when things are going well? What about when things aren't going well? Have you noticed? Take some time to observe what that voice in your head is saying: "I'm never going to make this team!" Or, more positively, "I'm on fire today!"

Our thoughts become actions. What I mean by that is if you are always thinking about things *not* working, you don't even need to say it out loud; you can just think it and then watch it transpire. And what are you saying to your child if you think it's going to be a long shot for him to make the team? "Well, gee, I doubt you'll make it." Or, "What do you think the coach is looking for in a player?"

The only six words parents should share with their child about their sports are: *I love to watch you play.*

That's it. With the rest? Lock it and keep it in your pocket! While many parents tell me they are just being honest, there's a big difference between being honest and being negative. It's simply not helpful to say something like, "The coach just doesn't like you; he likes Cynthia better, so you probably won't get much playing time this year." Even if it might be true, it's only going to further erode your athlete's confidence.

Build up, don't tear down, your kid.

Affirmations: "I Am" Statements
"I am" statements allow us to coach ourselves. And studies show that we can be the most powerful coaches we have. When you

coach yourself in the "I am..." voice, it can be as effective as having someone else give you feedback. The question, of course, is about the type of feedback you're giving yourself: is it positive or negative?

- I am powerful
- I am capable
- I am strong
- I am fierce
- I am loyal
- I am a hard worker

What are your or your athlete's "I am" statements? This would be a great dinner table conversation: write them down on Post-it notes and share them. Then put them up on your bathroom mirror and read them *out loud* to yourself in the morning or at night before bed. What you're saying to yourself about *you* matters. And when repeated consistently, it can start to shift how you feel, which will affect what choices you make about whether to take a risk or not, push yourself outside of your comfort zone, and be bold in your approach to sports and life.

You might try doing some in third person, like "LaTasha is strong..." because it accentuates us being seen by others in a positive light.

Daily Journaling

Four-time USA Volleyball Olympian Reid Priddy didn't start out as a ringer. Despite being undersized as an outside hitter at 6'4", his hard work and ability to jump—41"—helped him reach the highest level in the volleyball world. In addition to playing in four Olympics, he played professionally overseas for 15 years in six countries.

When asked what his biggest keys to success were, without hesitation he said journaling.

"My journaling helped me get my thoughts out of my head and onto the page. I've been journaling over 20 years now. I can look back at a journal entry from a certain day and I can read what I was thinking before a match, then go back and watch it on YouTube." Writing ideas about what you are focusing on helps you prioritize and get clear on what you are doing well and where you can use room for improvement.

When he writes he focuses on three things:

- "This is who I am…"
- "This is what I am doing…"
- "This is why I am doing it…"

When the world feels overwhelming, taking control of your thoughts allows you to get a feedback loop that slows you down, which helps create clarity. Priddy also recommends watching video of your match play. You can learn a lot if you can see the patterns of what you are and aren't doing consistently.

Daily Rituals: Habit Stacking
Creating a ritual every morning helps your brain to know what to expect. Here is a version for you to get inspiration from and create your own. The *most* important part of this is that it comes from within, not from you adopting the most successful person in the world's morning routine. But it must be intentional and consistent.

5:30 AM: Rise—Get out of bed, brush teeth, etc.

Get coffee, tea, or water

Find a quiet place you can meditate/pray

5:40 AM: Meditate for 20 min.

6:00 AM: Journal about your day (as if it's already happened)

After you've written how you want your day to play out, write down three to five things you will accomplish that day (work out with trainer, go to practice, get extra reps in, eat clean, drink lots of water). Goals can be sports-related, school/business-related, even family- and fun-related.

6:20 AM: Go CRUSH it

Your Tribe of Five, Living or Dead. Who Is at Your Table?
If you could meet with anyone living or dead, whether you knew them or not, who would you invite to your table? Curious people learn from others. Success leaves clues! So even if it's not someone you can actually speak to, research what Hank Aaron would have said regarding your dilemma, or ask John Wooden's opinion on your situation. Be creative. There is so much access to leaders' insights through podcasts, videos, and books. Seek it out!

I have a 14-year-old client who dreams of playing football at his dad's alma mater, University of North Carolina at Chapel Hill. He often speaks to a family friend who played football at Stanford. What a tremendous resource to learn how he got to play at that level, what he focused on, and who he learned from. There are so many pieces of that which are transferrable.

Purging: Relationships, Email, Clothes, Social Media, Clutter
Sometimes we have friends or family members who mean well but are afraid to see us fail, so they say things that don't support us in taking risks and going for our dreams. For anyone in your life who is holding you back, try this cord-cutting exercise. Imagine there is a rope wrapped around your ankle and it is tethered to theirs. Now picture cutting that emotional rope.

Say to your loved one: "I love you. I bless you. I forgive you. I release you."

You need every ounce of focus, energy, and support to reach your High Hard Goals. If someone is weighing you down, even if it feels like it's even a breath of a headwind, let them go. Note: that doesn't mean cutting that person out of your life, just the negativity that's getting in the way of your goal-seeking.

Purging relationships like your kids' room (parents, you feel me!), or social media—whatever clutters your life. Even going on a short social-media diet, a hiatus of a few days to a week, can help. Notice how you feel after not focusing all your energy on others and what they are doing. Now you have more time to create and execute what *you* desire.

No. 5: Capabilities

Ninety-five percent of what we do is driven by our subconscious. So what are you—or what is you athlete—feeding the beast? Are you coming up with new ways to get better at your craft or are you focusing on why you're not going to make the team you want to make?

Focusing on what we *can* do and building those skills sets is critical. Olivia Colman is now a winner of Academy Awards and many other honors, but not so long ago she was a cleaner. In her acceptance speech when she won, at age 45, the 2019 Best Actress Academy Award for her role in *The Favourite*, she said, "For years I was a cleaner. And I loved that job! And every day I would look in the mirror and practice my acceptance speech. But never in my wildest dreams did I imagine it would one day come true. Look at this! This is never going to happen again." But it did. Multiple times for her. And the real lesson there is you can be happy what you're doing now *and* have dreams about what you'd like to do in the future.

All that time she was cleaning, Colman was building her capabilities as an actor. She didn't just sit around and hope and wish. She took steps to achieve that goal. Daily steps.

So, it's time for *you* to jump in. Pick one of the above and try it. Just like we had to use training wheels when we first jumped on a bike, don't expect perfection on the first or fifth time you try to meditate. But keep sampling, journaling, writing down your goals, and reflecting on your performances. Over time, you will continue to see small improvements. Even 1 percent improvement daily leads to massive gains over time.

This is my favorite part of the journey. So, let me know if I can help! Reach out to me through my website: www.Kirsten JonesInc.com.

CHAPTER TWELVE

MENTAL HEALTH, A NATION IN CRISIS

Keeping your kids' bodies, minds, and souls healthy, safe, and thriving

AT 14, I EXPERIENCED MY MOST PAINFUL MEMORY involving sports. A freshman, I attended a small school in rural Montana where I made the varsity basketball team. The juniors and seniors didn't like that a freshman not only had made the roster but was a starter, so they did everything they could to make my life miserable.

It started with little things, like upper-class teammates stealing the ball from me during warm-ups in practice and whispering behind my back. But it quickly escalated to them standing at the top of the "jock stairs" in the morning before school to spit on me, laughing with their male classmates at that "silly little freshman."

But here was the topper: they slashed the tires on our family's car.

No, I am *not* making this up. It got that bad. And, in some ways, worse. After practice one day in the locker room, out of earshot of the male coach, they cornered me to let me know that if I didn't bring food for the entire team on a six-hour bus ride to Friday's game, they'd see to it that I didn't get to play. In fact, they promised to get me kicked off the team. Scared and defenseless at this threatened "hazing," I ran out of the locker room only to find that some of the girls had already run ahead to the coach and told him I wasn't being a team player and following the "rules."

When I mentioned to him about their demand, he blew me off; after all, they were the upperclassmen, and I was only a freshman.

"Don't worry, Kirsten; when you're an upperclassman, you can treat the freshmen the same way."

I was speechless.

It also stung that the assistant coach, a woman I admired deeply and who had been my middle school basketball coach, didn't stand up to him and defend me. It's stuck with me 35 years later.

In other words, I understand how impactful the tween and teen years are in kids' lives and how important it is they feel not only seen but also heard and valued by their teammates—and, most importantly, by the adults in the room, the coaches. As we read about young athletes taking their lives and otherwise struggling with mental health issues, I understand how lonely it can get out there in sports world. I absolutely believe we as parents need to be sensitive to our children's "inner lives" that might not be obvious to others.

And that's not easy.

For example, I never told my folks a thing about what I was going through. I had a very happy, healthy relationship with my parents. We were very close. I respected both of them a great deal and trust was high. Family dinners were always a priority and nearly every evening there was an uncomfortable topic to discuss, because they believed in the importance of strong communication. Still, despite having a great environment for sharing, I never mentioned a word to either parent about the months of hazing until decades later.

But the incident has stayed with me as a reminder of the type of things that a young athlete might be going through—alone. If I wanted to be a part of the team, I needed to play along in their hazing game? That was the moment I promised myself I would never treat another teammate or friend the way they were treating me. I also promised myself to outwork all of them, become a better player, thereby proving them all wrong! My goal was clear. I was going to be an All-State player. I was hurt and humiliated that this coach valued keeping his upperclassmen happy over being equitable and fair to all his players.

It forged my outlook on what being a good teammate means and perhaps now with the wisdom of hindsight, made me realize what the silver lining was. It helped me not only to pursue playing DI volleyball in college but to find Nike and eventually to pursue a career as a Peak Performance Coach. I aspire to help others avoid what I went through, or anything remotely similar, by giving them tools to address issues as they arise.

If you can take the lemons you are given (life experience!) and make lemonade (growth), you'll go far beyond anyone else's limitations for you. And yet it's becoming clearer that some athletes are feeling an unprecedented amount of stress; at times, they see no way out.

Stanford's Katie Meyer was a great daughter, sister, friend, and teammate. She was the star standout goalkeeper for the 2019 NCAA National Championship women's soccer team. In February of 2022, everyone was blindsided by news that she had committed suicide.

After a phone call from her daughter, Gina Meyer said she and her husband had zero indication that anything was wrong with Katie. In fact, they were making spring break plans. Katie was planning to come home for a few days before heading to Mexico with friends. Gina Meyer had no idea that Katie was grieving some disciplinary charges a friend was facing from the university. The family was close, yet Katie never mentioned the charges to her parents.

"When [things get difficult], sometimes [college-aged students] think they can 'adult' and they think they can handle it, but sometimes they can't," Meyer said. "They may need extra support from someone, someone checking in on them, someone saying, 'Hey, can I help you with this? What can we do? How can I help you?'"

This hit me hard. When I reflect back to my Montana story, I have no idea why my 14-year-old self decided that I needed to hide my situation from my parents. Maybe I just figured everyone went through their own version of this and it was something I needed to handle. My reason for not sharing wasn't because I didn't think my parents would believe me.

Decades later, why did Katie decide not to share her situation with her parents or a coach or a professor? And why was it something she thought she couldn't get through?

While we will never know what made her decide to take her own life, what we do know is there are important touchpoints we need to be having with our kids both while at home and after they fly out of the nest.

As a sports parenting coach, I've heard far too many stories similar to mine. If not hazing, per se, it's a coach who's not helping to support and develop all of the players. One parent relayed to me how her 16-year-old—and 6'1"—daughter, who was new to the sport of volleyball, had been written off by the coach within the first few months of the season. She wasn't allowed to join in drills (or very minimally allowed to join) and spent more of her time during practice just shagging balls and helping other athletes get better. When she asked if she could do the drills, she was told, "No, you just need to shag." Clearly this coach had decided who he wanted to invest in and who he felt wasn't worth allowing to even run a drill in practice.

Coaches are working to win. Despite how much money and time you invest, most clubs and high school coaches will tell you their top priority is championships. Their clubs and their jobs are on the line if they can't produce winning results.

Putting the best team on the floor during a game or match is understandable. Still, not allowing players to develop hinders the individual athlete, both mentally and physically, and ultimately hurts the team. Because when someone doesn't make it to the next match and the player who has only been shagging balls is called to go into play, she's not prepared to compete. And that's one hundred percent on the coach.

A coach's job is to develop and support *all* of the players on the team, not just the ones he likes or thinks have the most potential. They are teenagers. They aren't going to the Olympics any time soon! It galls me to consider all the time, cost, and effort these kids are making just to get to practice three or four days a week. In the case of the neglected newcomer, the family lived more than 90 minutes away from the practice facility. Three hours a day in the car only to not learn and develop? Almost as unacceptable as a coach who looks the other way at hazing.

If you've been a (sports) parent for long, you've probably realized that not every season goes according to plan for your child. Stuff happens. Coaches neglect certain kids. Circumstances shift. Kids change. Ankles break.

None of which you can control. But you can control your reaction to it. "We can't control the wind," goes the adage, "but we can adjust our sails." Children have a difficult enough time with this mental-health game on their own; they desperately need us in their corners, especially when mistreatment is involved.

It's normal to be concerned about your kids' playing time; it's not normal to pay to have a plane fly a banner over the baseball field calling out the coaches. Be reasonable. Don't major in the minors.

That said, don't overlook the "majors," like when a coach is downright mean, derogatory, or punitive to the point of crushing a child's love of the sport. Great coaches have the opportunity to ignite a flame for an athlete. Many are the catalyst for a kid developing a lifelong passion for a sport. But bad coaches can do just the opposite: contribute to such a devastating experience with a coach that they quit playing the sport entirely and never come back to it.

My son had that happen with soccer at age 13. One spiteful coach was able to eliminate any interest he had in ever playing again—and this was a kid who had played it for eight years and loved the game deeply.

Beyond bad coaches, other stressors can put your child's mental health in jeopardy: we've seen a growing post-COVID surge of anxiety, depression, and increasing rates of suicide. The pressure that coaches, administration, and athletes feel to win seeps into everything college athletes are now feeling way beyond the games they play. Understanding this pressure is important for parents.

According to the Society for Adolescent Health and Medicine (SAHM), here are some potential warning signs that it could be time to seek help for your child's depression:

- Social isolation, avoiding social situations
- No longer interested in activities they used to enjoy
- Decline in school performance, even though they used to be a good student

- "My son stays in his room all day"
- "Our daughter is always angry"
- Agitation and constant fidgeting
- Changes in appetite and weight
- Self-harm, such as cutting
- Decline in grooming and self-care habits
- Risky behavior, including abusing alcohol or drugs as a form of self-medication

Of course, the tricky part is being able to differentiate between what is "normal" teen behavior (the attitude in the morning on the way to the bus because you had the gall to wake them up five minutes early) and what is depressive behavior. If you find yourself seeing multiple of the above signs, particularly for weeks on end, don't hesitate, get help. Start with your pediatrician and get a referral from them.

CONNECTION

Your teenager will benefit from having friends and mentors outside of their immediate family who they can confide in. An Australian client of mine whose son is playing DI basketball in the United States called me in a panic recently. Her son had some underlying health conditions that were acting up, she felt like he wasn't thriving, and only one thing was clear: "He doesn't want his mum flying over to fix everything." She kind of laughed, but I could hear the quiver in her voice that she wasn't feeling comforted with him halfway around the globe and not being able to see him and the situation with her own eyes.

She mentioned the team's athletic trainer offered to connect him with their sports psychologists but was unsure if this was a good idea. In my opinion, any resources that can help our athletes feel seen and heard, particularly once they are away from home, can be helpful. She completely agreed that she didn't want to overstep her bounds but acknowledged that because he was a rookie, he wasn't at all proactive in letting the coach know he wasn't feeling well. In fact, in one practice he collapsed on the floor because he wasn't hydrated, and the coach accused him of partying too much. While that might be the case for many freshmen in college, she knew he had been so sick because of his disease that he hadn't been able to lift his head off the pillow, much less chug a bottle of beer.

Don't wait. Get help before there's an issue. I encourage all teens to find a neutral source to confide in. It may just be a one-time touch base, but it could also grow into a relationship over the years. I have one client in Chicago I won't hear from for months and then out of the blue, he'll schedule a call to check in and get a "tune up."

Many college programs these days have sports psychologists on staff, but if they don't, encourage your athlete to ask the coaching staff. Lots of coaches I speak to understand that while they are there to support the athletes, there are times when the kids don't want to talk to them about anything personal or private or anything that might jeopardize playing time. They realize that is completely understandable and are usually relieved to hear the kids are interested in connecting with another peer or adult to get some counsel.

Alliances could be:

- **An athlete.** It could be someone just one or two steps ahead of your child. Someone who recently went through something similar to what your child is going through now can be a good resource for "next steps."
- **A coach.** When trust is high and the relationship is solid, a coach can be extremely helpful as a sounding board for your athlete.

- **A sports psychologist or performance coach.** I often tell my clients, "I'm Switzerland." I'm here to help cheer you on and help you get what you want. *Here is your mom and dad's point of view; what's yours?* Teens are relieved, and encouraged, when they are heard.

Tools for Dealing with Stress

Proactively create routines that help athletes develop positive habits to help them deal with stress. As they say, it is better to be a thermostat than a thermometer. *You* set the temperature of a thermostat. Maybe it will vary by a degree or two, but if you are the thermometer, you are just reacting to whatever weather is around you. One minute you're feeling a balmy 65 degrees, but within seconds adversity arises and you're a scalding 95 degrees.

The worst time to try and put out the fire is when the building is engulfed in flames.

The fight-or-flight response kicks in and the result usually isn't positive. Stress makes us stupid. If we can slow the reaction time down to what's coming at us, it allows us to choose our reaction instead of feeling as if we're drinking through a firehose.

Whenever he got shot at, Neo, in the movie *The Matrix* could bend time and watch the bullet flying at him in slow motion. That's what using these tools and techniques regularly can do for you. Even though I went through these in depth in Chapter 11, I need to mention them again. Because for someone, it's literally a matter of life or death:

- Meditation
- Mindfulness
- Yoga
- Journaling

- Podcasts/books/music
- Working with a counselor/sports psychologist or coach
- Breath work
- Surrounding yourself with people who support you. Purging those who don't. Nothing, of course, makes a young person foolproof from stresses that can lead to tragic decisions. At the same time, with so much on the line, we dare not take the matter lightly.

PART IV

STRATEGY III: APPRECIATING TEAM & COACH DYNAMICS

CHAPTER THIRTEEN

PUTTING WE OVER ME

Emphasizing the "greater good" of team

MY FRIEND AND FORMER HIGH SCHOOL TEAMMATE, Karen Deden, is no stranger to winning. She is arguably the best women's basketball player to ever come out of the state of Montana. She was an All-Pac-10 selection, leading Washington to four straight NCAA appearances. And, as a coach, she led her alma mater, Sentinel High School, to Class AA state championships in 2012, 2013, and 2014.

"Who was the toughest player you ever coached in your 21 years?" I asked her.

She didn't hesitate in selecting a 5'0" point guard named Brittany Wulf, who was an integral part of two of those state titles.

Karen told me straight up, "She practiced harder than any player I ever had. She would go to the YMCA after practice every day to get another hour of reps in. She never complained once about her playing time. She was our energizer bunny. She was always positive no matter what. I had five DI athletes on that team, and she made it because of who she was to us. She was the epitome of selfless.

"The team was always first. She put in so much time and poured her heart and soul into the game. Honestly, I felt bad that I couldn't get her more playing time. She got in for a few minutes per game, but it was limited because her physical stature. What was never a problem was the size of her heart.

"You could ask any player on that team during those years who was the hardest worker and they would all say Britt. She did her best every day to make her teammates better. She truly was one of a kind. Amazing dribbler. Always there for everyone and had a great sense of humor."

As parents, of course, we want the best for our kids. And sometimes in our tunnel vision to help support them in their dreams, we make bad decisions. We overreach regarding a coach. We "under listen" regarding our child. Ideally, we want our child to give 100 percent, overcome whatever barriers they face, and become the quintessential team player.

Austin Hatch was such a player. Hatch faced tremendous adversity multiple times but refused to let it define him. According to MIT statistician Arnold Barnett, the odds of surviving a plane crash resulting in one or more fatalities is one in 3.4 million. Austin Hatch survived *two*, the odds of which are one in more than 11 quadrillion. In a span of eight years, Hatch survived two plane crashes that claimed the five people closest to him.

In 2003, eight-year-old Austin lost his mother, younger brother, and older sister in a plane crash that he survived. In 2011, just days after making his commitment to play basketball at University of Michigan, he survived a second plane crash in which he lost his dad and stepmom.

The second left him with brain damage, and doctors feared he'd never walk again. When Austin awoke from a medically induced coma, Michigan coach John Beilein was there in the hospital room. Coach assured him he'd be with him the entire way, no matter how long it took.

Austin would have to re-learn how to walk and talk again. He would never be able to fulfill the dream he had as a young boy to become a Wolverine legend on the court, but ironically, his legacy is arguably much greater despite him not getting much playing time.

When I had him on my *#RaisingAthletes* podcast back in March 2019, he said:

> I never would have never chosen what I went through, losing my family in the tragic events that I did. The way I see it I had two very bad days, but I can't let those define me. In the moment, I realized there were hurdles I had to overcome physically and mentally to get back to full strength, but there was also nothing I could do to change the past.
>
> The opportunity was for me to embrace what was in front of me which started with me showing gratitude to Coach. His believing in me, sticking by me, and allowing me to be a part of his legendary program was something I never took for granted. Of course I would rather been an impact player on the court, but when that wasn't an option, I focused on what was possible. And that was for me to be the best teammate. I figured if I helped get the bags from the bus to the gym or hotel faster than anyone else, that would allow the guys to focus on what they needed to do to win. So that's what I did. And I loved every minute of it.

I was blown away by the complete absence of selfishness, anger, or bitterness about what had happened to him. Where was the, "Why me? Why did I have to go through this?" It would have been completely understandable. But he spent zero time blaming anyone else or holding grudges. He was, and is, a man who lives to serve, and that has continued far beyond the basketball court.

In 2018, he married a fellow Michigan athlete and the woman of his dreams, Abby Cole. He considers himself "the luckiest person alive." He owns his own company, Overcome It. He writes, speaks, and inspires teams and companies about overcoming adversity.

"Life is not about what we do for ourselves," Hatch says, "It's about how we impact others."

Parents, the best thing you can do for your child is to model that concept to him or her. Walk the talk. It's one thing to tell your child to be a good sport or to work hard, but it is far more impactful to show them in your actions. Let them see both the good and bad decisions you make.

My co-host Susie Walton has a saying: "If you don't make mistakes often, *pretend.* Get off at the wrong exit and exclaim out loud for your child to hear, 'Well, look at that! I made an oopsie.' When you admit your own mistakes, you are letting your child know that when they make a mistake, it's OK. In fact, it's more than OK, it's how we are supposed to do life, by learning from our mistakes. Unfortunately, not all parents are up to speed on this lesson."

I was recently at an "AAU live period" boys basketball event at which college coaches are allowed to come to recruit high school athletes. There were 20-plus college coaches on the baseline looking for talent to add to their roster. It was the last game of the day and there were 20 seconds remaining on the clock. My son's team was up by four points. A time-out was called by the opposing team. A dad from that team decided it was his opportunity to berate one of the officials.

"Hey ref, want me to teach you how to count? Do you know how to count to 10? I can teach you if you want."

It was hot in the gym; it was 9:30 PM, the end of the last game of a very long day of hoops. The referee stayed remarkably calm and moved closer to the stands. Looking the dad in the eyes, he quietly stated, "You know you can leave if you'd like."

The dad wasn't having it and just kept going. He kept talking over the ref and wouldn't let down. The ref kept his composure and reiterated his point. But pretty soon, a woman sitting next the low-class spectator stood and got in the ref's face as well.

The time-out ended and the players were ready to finish the last remaining seconds of the game. But the game couldn't begin again because of the altercation. Eventually, the ref from the far side of the court and one of the tournament officials had to get involved. Obviously out of patience, most college coaches left the gym.

I felt sorry for the man's son. Hey, pal, this isn't about you! This is about letting your kid play. I did eventually hear a mom from that same team shout, "You're only hurting our kids. Just let them play." But the dad's actions, his choice to model bad behavior sent the message to his son that when something doesn't go your way, protest. Object. Throw a fit. And make sure everyone in the gym knows what you think.

Earlier that same night, I had seen similar behavior from one of the players, a guy who likely had a dad just like the other one I mentioned. He was a seven-foot-tall athletic kid but was having an off night and getting frustrated that his team was losing. He started talking smack to his opponent. I could see the guy guarding him trying to not respond, but eventually it got the best of him, and he just turned to the kid.

"Look at the scoreboard. We're up by 30."

The seven-footer didn't like being called out and took a full swing at his opponent—in front of college coaches who were there to potentially recruit him. Yikes.

In both of those situations, if I was a college coach, I'd figure out who the son of the ref-rippin' father was and who the seven-footer was, and I'd cross them off the list. There's just too much talent to deal with any of those shenanigans. What a waste. You know that athlete had worked hard for this opportunity. You can imagine he was feeling the pressure of the moment, but he chose the wrong way to respond.

So, what can you as parents do to model the "we, not me" philosophy of teamwork to your young athletes—and not shoot down your kid's chance for a scholarship?

- **First, be on time.** We're not looking for perfection here, but it does require planning. My rule of thumb is adding 20–30 minutes to the estimated travel time. I can guarantee you you're never going to hear a coach complain, "Yes, but she was *always* 30 minutes early and it was so annoying!" In fact, I often hear the opposite, because consistently showing up early is such an anomaly. "Because Jessie was always early, she was able to get extra reps and was always ready to lend a hand getting ready for practice. I not only saw rapid improvement, but was more likely to play her when the opportunity presented itself." Thirty minutes is early. Fifteen minutes is on time. Showing up the minute practice is supposed to start is late. Be early. Every day.

- **Second, model a strong work ethic and effort.** I'm guessing Brittany, from the start of this chapter, never told Coach Deden she was going to the YMCA after practice. The other girls on the team did that for her. Focus on what you can control and let the rest go. She has 100 percent control over how hard she works and how often she works. So does your child.

- **Third, don't "protect" yourself with excuses.** NBA legend and LA Lakers star Kobe Bryant famously practiced four times per day, twice what the Lakers required. "I intentionally worked out twice as much as everyone else so that mentally I knew that there was no way my opponent (or any of my teammates) was going to beat me." My husband, Evan, was the senior brand manager for Nike Basketball from 2004 to 2007. He once had a meeting with Kobe to talk about Bryant's future with the Swoosh. When Evan asked him how he would explain his work ethic, he said it was simple; "There are people who have doubted me. Their doubt fuels my drive. In order to not let their hate hold me back, I created a 'wall of pain.' Any time anyone made a disparaging comment about me, I would write it down on my wall and assign a workout to it. Not a leader: Baselines x 20… Too young: Lunges 15 x 4… Uncoachable: Tricep press 10 x 4." And on and on. You get the idea. He reveled in the chance to add any hater to his wall. His work ethic was so strong.

- **Fourth, watch your body language.** When I meet with teams or individual athletes and ask them to rate themselves on a scale of 1–10 on a list of things that require zero talent, "body language" always scores low. "I know I slump my shoulders whenever I don't make the right play. I look down at the floor and I wish it would swallow me." When I ask why they do that, most aren't sure but when pressed admit they want their teammates (or parents) to know that they feel bad they made a mistake. "What's the most powerful pose you can make?" I ask them. The answer may not surprise you, but it's funny. Standing with your legs shoulder width apart, your head held high, and hands on your hips, like Wonder Woman. This is the most powerful pose you can make. In fact, it is called the

"Wonder Woman" pose. And social psychologist Amy Cuddy claims that when you stand like that, it raises testosterone, lowers the stress hormone cortisol, and helps reset your brain. She argues that it leads to "hormonal changes that configure your brain to basically be either assertive, confident, and/or comfortable."

- **Fifth, exude energy, attitude, and passion.** For those who have a goal, it's not always about the glory that comes with it. One such example of this is from Sam Beskind, a Stanford men's basketball walk-on who explains in an essay what it truly means to compete daily with zero guarantees of playing time: You say to yourself, "It's going to be a long road." Give your all, knowing it may never be enough. Turn down scholarship opportunities and instead pursue your dream. It won't be easy, but it will be worth it. Remember your sixth grade goal, "Earn an athletic scholarship to Stanford." Give your all, knowing it may never be enough. Lean on your family when you feel lost, discouraged, and want to go home. Arrive on campus months behind everyone else. Be unafraid by the size, strength, and speed of those around you. Embrace the nervous excitement instead of feeling fear. Each day try to find a single thing you did right; some days you won't be able to find anything at all. When it all seems to fail, remember that your worth does not reside in performance.
- **Sixth, embody humility.** Do you see others excel without putting in the work? Life isn't fair, my friend; learn that early. Rejoice in others' success, don't envy it. Be your teammates' biggest fan. Cheer so loud you lose your voice. Read books to help embrace your role. Be a willful servant and feel entitled to nothing. Carry bags through the airport and warm-up your teammates, and do both with a smile. Embody humility.
- **Seventh, be coachable.** Do extra and be prepared. A friend's son was the last kid to be picked for a summer travel baseball

team. The coach told him from the get-go that playing time would come hard and he was right. The kid hardly ever played. But nobody worked harder in practice. Nobody complained less. Nobody chattered more from the dugout to support his teammates. Tijuan was always first to the field. He would ask coach if he could warm up his arm with Coach or get some batting practice in before the other guys showed up, knowing full well he probably wasn't going to see the field or get a chance at bat that week. At summer's end, in the championship tourney, a player got hurt and Tijuan was the replacement. In his first at-bat he scorched an RBI single to right field to ignite a game-winning rally. Still, he finished the season with hardly any playing time. "Years later, my friend ran into the coach of that team. 'You know,' the coach said, 'of all the kids I coached, your son was my favorite.'"

One of the themes of this book is not just raising good athletes, but empowered people. Not just good athletes, but good sports. The type of kid who might not stand out in a box score but will be successful in whatever he or she pursues.

Mom, Dad, you can help make that happen.

CHAPTER FOURTEEN

THE ROLE OF A VOLUNTEER COACH

The importance of keeping it simple

FEET FACING THE TARGET.
  Fingertips.
  Wrinkle wrist.
  Cookie jar.

The words rolled off CJ's tongue as if he'd just learned them, as if they were as fresh as a bakery's Boston Cream doughnut. Over the phone, he was recounting a memory to me and my husband about how Evan had first taught him, a kindergartener at the time, to shoot a basketball in a YMCA league. Now, 14 years later, CJ had called us in excitement from Boston, where he was a freshman on the Boston University basketball team.

"I don't believe it," he said. "One of the seniors pulled me aside after practice. 'Hey, CJ,' he said. 'How'd you get to be such a great shooter?' A senior!"

The question, CJ told us, caught him off guard. "I wasn't expecting one of the seniors to ask *me* for advice. But I was thrilled that he did. Without thinking I immediately remembered what Dad taught me in the driveway so many years ago."

One, feet facing your target.

Two, the ball shouldn't be resting on the palm of your hand, it should be balancing lightly on your fingertips.

Three, cock your hand back so you can see the wrinkles in your wrist when you are launching the ball.

Four, when you go to shoot, reach high, like you're trying to get into the cookie jar on the shelf to snag a delicious treat.

"While trying to help my teammate identify a few bad habits he was trying to break," he told us, "I was reminded of the good ones I needed a little refresher on. I realized I'd gotten lazy in my shooting. This was the perfect reminder that whenever something isn't working, always go back to the fundamentals."

It's true, out of the mouths of babes sometimes comes great wisdom: parents, it's possible that at times you're going to be doing double duty—not only being a mom or dad to a young one trying to negotiate the slippery slopes of youth sports but also being a coach. And even if you're not going to coach in an official capacity, you may well be teaching your child the basics of some sport.

Hint: keep it simple. Teach the fundamentals. Don't suddenly think you're former Duke coach Mike Krzyzewski or Connecticut's Geno Auriemma. Just be yourself and teach the kids the fundamentals of the game. It's in the kids' best interest. It's in *your* best interest.

Here, let me explain: Evan learned the keys to being a sharpshooter back in a middle school summer basketball camp in Eugene, Oregon, from South Eugene High coach Dean Stepp. Evan eventually went on to play for Coach Stepp in high school and then play in college at DIII Johns Hopkins University and

DII University of California-Davis, where he was known for his ability to drain the three. In fact, he and I met when he was playing as one of two foreigners for a professional basketball team in Budapest, Hungary. When our kids—besides CJ , 22, we have Parker, 19 and Kylie, 16—were old enough and Evan first considered how to best teach them proper technique, the first thing that popped into his head was the fundamentals he'd learned about shooting from Coach Stepp.

Feet facing the target. Fingertips. Wrinkle wrist. Cookie jar.

Evan began coaching CJ in a National Junior Basketball (NJB) league when he was nine. Evan's teams never ran complicated out-of-bounds plays or multiple offenses. Kids at that age don't even understand the concept of traveling, much less a double-down screen to the post. Knowing this, Evan focused on teaching the kids the fundamentals of the game: dribbling, passing, shooting, and where to be on the floor. The basics.

At that age, kids are like a swarm of bees: like in soccer at that age, wherever the swarm is, count on the ball being in the center of it. It can be a game-changer just teaching kids how spreading out from their teammates can open up all sorts of possibilities for wide-open shots.

Keep It Simple

Several years later, when we lived in Buffalo, New York, Evan was too busy at work to serve as a head coach but became an assistant for CJ's sixth-grade team. The head coach was a kind man and the father of two middle school-aged boys. He had never played the game himself, but that didn't stop him from drawing up four different offenses, two defenses, and three out-of-bounds plays. I was like: *Really?* Hey, some of these kids were still trying to figure out offense from defense, much less trying to master a full-court press with trapping guards.

The coach spent most of his practices trying to teach them set plays, convinced that such sophistication would be the team's key to success. They'd win the sixth-grade championships, he apparently figured, and, when the season was over, he'd take his family to Disneyworld—if he could break away from the ESPN interviews. You get the idea: when it came to connecting to 12-year-olds, he was—with all the best intentions—living in an alternate universe.

"Duke! Run Duke!" he'd yell from the bench. "Orange 51! Orange 51!"

You could almost see the thought bubbles above the boys' heads: *Orange 51? What the heck is that? Hey, I wonder if we'll get to go for ice cream after the game!*

Toward season's end, Evan respectfully asked the coach if he could talk to the boys before a game. No problem.

"Three things," he told the team. "Talk to each other, space out, and be aggressive. Any questions?"

The kids stared back at him like *he* was from an alternate universe.

"That's all?" asked one kid.

"That's all."

"What about our plays?"

"Don't worry about plays. Focus on communication, spacing yourselves apart from one another, and staying aggressive."

When one of them was doing something wrong, Evan, during a time-out, would bend his 6'5" frame down so he could look the kid in the eye. Then he'd tell the boy one thing he wanted the player to work on in that moment. Just one thing. And a simple "one" at that.

"In the heat of battle, kids don't need three or four things being yelled at them," he'd say. "That's overwhelming. Eventually, they just shut down."

Imagine if you were preparing for a huge presentation in front of your company and as you're ready to walk up on stage, your boss air-bombs you with "three things you definitely shouldn't mention and four things you better not forget."

Wait, what? Uh...hey...help!

You'd feel overwhelmed. You might even shut down. Welcome to the world of too many kids in youth sports these days.

In Los Angeles, four girls on the 17LA team were out sick for a Premier Volleyball League (PVL) tournament. Bad news for them, but good news for four players who normally don't get much playing time, including a girl named Rena.

She was nervous. Rena was one of those backup players. She'd gradually improved over the season but had never gotten much of a chance to test herself in an actual match.

Encouragement Goes a Long Way

It had been a long day. The team had already played three tight matches and Rena's play had been inconsistent at best, shaky at worst. Everyone was tired and the hour delay while waiting for the championship match to start wasn't helping anyone's patience or nerves.

"OK, let's warm up!" the head coach said to her team.

The girls looked lethargic; the coach annoyed. The second assistant, knowing they were facing a rock-star team they often played in the finals and were running on empty, huddled the players.

"Girls, did you know this is the *last* match you're going to play in 2020? This is it. You're not going to play again this year."

The girls perked up a bit.

"Have a look over there at Long Beach Mizuno. They're all fired up and ready to beat us. They look forward to every chance they get to play us. How do you want to end your final match of this year?"

That's all that needed saying. The energy switch had been flipped. A new spirit infused the warm-up session. This team was ready to end the year on a high!

Rena started the game but just couldn't get her momentum rolling. The head coach subbed her out.

"You gotta get up quicker in the middle!" the head coach barked with staccato angst. "And on defense, you're too slow and they are hitting right past you."

On the bench, Rena's head slumped forward into her hands in frustration; she was bummed that she was letting down her coach. The second assistant coach noted the look of despair on Rena's face it and slid down next to her on the bench. This wasn't the assistant's first rodeo. She'd been a collegiate and Olympic player. Seen a lot. Better than that, *knew* a lot, particularly about what might be going on in the minds of players like Rena.

"How ya feeling?" she asked the girl.

Rena wouldn't make eye contact.

"I have to get up quicker in the middle," she mumbled. "And on defense, I'm too slow; they're hitting right by me."

"Look," said the assistant, "I know you got that feedback and Coach is right, but let's talk about what you can do to fix it."

Rena looked at the coach sideways. "Fix it?"

"Yeah, if you make some small adjustments, you'll be able to contribute next time you're in the game."

Rena's eyes lit up with a glimmer of hope. Until now, she'd been crushed by a sense of failure. But now, just a few simple words had changed her perspective. Until now the only things she could focus on what she was doing *wrong*. Now the assistant was offering her advice on how she could do things *right*. Suddenly, it seemed possible to her, the idea of her doing something to help the team. Relief washed over Rena's face. When it came time to sub in, she stood taller, and jogged eagerly onto the floor, as if a completely different player.

The head coach immediately noticed. She looked down the bench, smiled at the assistant, and mouthed the words, "Thank you."

Rena didn't suddenly pound balls with Olympian power and make diving save after diving save, but she made some key plays and helped the team win the championship. Later that night, the assistant's phone rang. It was Rena's mother.

"Thank you so much," she said.

"For what?"

"You were so kind to give Rena positive reinforcement at such a stressful moment. Thank you so much for taking the time to help her through it and help her come out the other side stronger."

Sometimes, parents, the little stuff is the big stuff.

It's not always about the offense you run or the talent you have. Sometimes it's about the basics. About that one moment when you shift a child's perspective just a smidgeon—enough to make her believe in herself again. Sometimes it's about the physical part of the game and sometimes about the mental part of the game. *Let's talk about what you can fix.* At any rate, whether you're coaching in the heat of battle or at home trying to teach a daughter to grip a softball bat, remember the fundamentals.

Advice for volunteer coaches:

- **Memorize these four letters: K.I.S.S.** Keep. It. Simple. Stupid. Sure, it's a cliché, but it's also true. Kids don't need complicated offenses or defenses at age nine or 10. If they understand the general rules of the game and you keep it light and fun, they will keep coming back for more.
- **Teach the simple fundamentals of the game.** Use a metaphor or quick analogy that can help a player remember what you taught them long after they've finished playing for you. *Feet facing the target. Fingertips. Wrinkle wrist. Cookie jar.*

- **Don't overcomplicate things.** Kids under 13 don't need to run complicated offenses or defenses. Help them learn basic techniques, how to carry their body, and how to run, throw, and catch properly.
- **Answer the basic questions kids will have about their sport.** What do the terms offense, defense, free throw and full-court press mean? How many quarters are there? How should we react when we lose? (Hint, you're modeling it—for better or worse.) How should we react when we win? (Yup, modeling there, too). What should we do when one of the players from the other team falls down? (Help them up). And, in basketball, what should we do you if we foul out? (Hold your head up and high-five your teammates before you leave the floor.)
- **Rally the team in a positive way.** Keep your players focused on the goal. Help them keep the game in perspective. *This is our chance to beat our archrival! End the season on a high!*
- **Give positive feedback to players one-on-one.** When you note something that can help a player improve his or her game, offer one or two ideas, face to face, with a positive spin. Don't overwhelm them with myriad things to fix while they're running down the floor.

Volunteer coaching is a wonderful opportunity to change young lives. Like teachers, coaches have the power to influence the trajectory of a child's life. I've seen in it my job as a life coach, in my experience as a DI volleyball player and coaching young athletes, and in my role as a podcast co-host. Something you impart to a child can help that child grow into a healthy, positive adult.

And it all begins with the fundamentals, with reaching for the cookie jar.

Chapter Fifteen

TRANSACTIONAL VERSUS TRANSFORMATIONAL COACHING

Understanding the kind of coaching you should want— and what to flee from

"What do you consider transactional coaching?" I asked a current high school boys' basketball coach at a well-respected prep school.

He said his mind immediately went to an experience he had with a coach as a high school player. "Get on the line, Andy. If you can't follow my directions, you can put on that pink T-shirt. Since you're going to act like a girl you might as well dress like one. You can run until you figure out how to do the drill I'm asking you to do." Despite that happening more than two decades earlier, you could tell it still stung. *My way or the highway.*

"His entire strategy was to wear you down. Humiliate you in front of your teammates. He'd pick on your shot selection or your defense. He never gave reasoning and he never followed up with what he did want to see from you. It was mostly a self-serving way to show you who was in charge. It was belittling and demoralizing and I have never forgotten how it made me feel."

That story may sound like outright bullying, because it is. It is also a strategy some coaches use to get what they want. Lead with the stick and "encourage" everyone to follow. As parents we, of course, want to protect our kids. And given the current nature of the highly involved parenting culture, you may feel this story isn't as relevant as it was 20 years old. But it is because it goes to the principle of values.

This chapter is about building awareness about what type of coach you are choosing to pair your child with and whether their leadership style and your child's personality and learning style are aligned.

Sometimes we can get so enamored with the legend of a coach and the banners on the gym wall that we overlook a fundamental question: Will he or she not only help make my child a better athlete but a better person? Not all winning coaches will.

Transactional Leaders

In 2011, former Syracuse University standout and NFL star-turned-leadership-coach Joe Ehrman wrote a book detailing the pros and cons of transactional ("I'm God; you're not") versus transformational (think UCLA legendary coach John Wooden) coaching. Through years of doing clinics with athletes and their parents, Ehrman heard hundreds of stories about transactional coaches. So many, in fact, he was able to put them into five buckets: dictators, bullies, narcissists, saints, and misfits.

I'd like to relate each of these to athletes I've known.

Dictators, Bullies, and Narcissists: *My Way or the Highway*

Some coaches' biggest fear is that they will be perceived as too soft. Most likely somewhere in their upbringing by either a parent/guardian or a coach (or both), they were ruled with an iron fist and there was very little allowance to show emotions.

Jill, a former neighbor, called me one day out of the blue a few years ago to tell me her oldest son was now a sophomore in college and rowing in a highly competitive college program. Dan has always loved rowing. Getting the opportunity to row for a USA National team coach who was also this school's college coach was a dream come true, or so he thought, until he got there.

In crew, it's all about your "ERG time," i.e., indoor rowers are also known as ergometers or erg for short. When he first got to school they were all tested on the erg. In order to get into an actual boat on the water, you needed to hit a certain time while rowing on the erg. Many athletes struggled early on, Dan included. But with daily workouts and lots of reps he started to see his improvement in his times. He knew he wasn't there yet, but what confused him was that the coach had singled him out in a team of dozens. One day the coach moved the erg out of the boat house and put it on the dock. While the rest of the athletes were allowed to get into the boats and out onto the water, he was left there alone, humiliated for everyone to see that he hadn't made the cut to get in the boats.

"He was doing the work," his mother said. "He'd call home and tell me he was training hard to meet the standards, but the coach spent most workouts publicly humiliating him in front of his teammates. It just breaks my heart to hear him speak about a sport he used to love so much, knowing he's not living up to this coach's levels, but feels powerless to do anything. He keeps telling me, 'It's so painful, Mom, I don't understand why he's singled me out,' and that is the worst thing you can hear as a parent."

Daniel's family is Mormon and he was getting ready to do his two-year mission. Jill was calling me to ask what I thought they should do. Should they report it to the athletic director or just ride out the season and look to leave it behind when Dan left for his mission?

It's hard to know how to handle an injustice when we see it happening to our child, even if technically they are now of legal age. Knowing when to back off or when to step in if you're fearful your child's safety may be at risk. I recommended they ask Dan what he wanted to do. He is the one who had to deal with this coach daily. As parents, our tendency is to swoop in to solve a problem; unfortunately, especially when our kids get older, the best play is to support them but let them lead the response.

Narcissists: "Me, Me, Me...It's All About Me."

The dictionary definition of a narcissist is a person who has an excessive interest in or admiration of themselves. Someone who is strictly focused on their feelings, needs, and desires without cause or concern for others.

A sign of a narcissistic coach is someone who would work to engender themselves to the players. Someone who makes plans and crosses personal boundaries with their players to get to know them. This makes the players feel like they really care because they are asking so much about them, their dating lives, school, and about who their friends are and social gossip. Then when things get stressful, they will use this information against the kids.

"Now I see why he broke up with you! You're lazy." They see it as a way to motivate. In reality, it crosses lines and it feels not only violating but demoralizing. Here are a few signs to help you identify this type of coach:

- Grandiose sense of self-importance.
- Lives in a fantasy world that supports their delusions of grandeur.
- Needs constant praise and admiration.
- Sense of entitlement.
- Exploits others without guilt or shame.
- Frequently demeans, intimidates, bullies, or belittles others.
- I've seen so many of these coaches that it's all but impossible to describe just one. The bottom line is that they are ego-driven and not other-driven. Beware of them. They will not have your son or daughter's best interest in mind, and they will not make the experience fun.

Saints: "Only I Can Save You"

Coaches get into the profession of coaching for different reasons. Some are former players who loved the game so much they decided to teach the next generation, some had a great mentor who showed them the way and that inspired them to follow in their footsteps, while others knew they wanted to teach and found that they could earn a little extra money by coaching, too. Whatever the reason, many coaches I have spoken to over the years have told me they ultimately decided to coach because they wanted to give back.

But as altruistic as that reasoning is, even that can sometimes go bad. What happens when you get a coach who thinks it's their role to save everyone around them? Here are signs of the rescue-type coaches:

- A coach who is getting unnecessarily involved in their athletes' lives and is trying to insert themselves into helping them fix whatever is wrong.
- A coach who makes excessive personal sacrifices such as time, money, personal space on a consistent basis.

- A coach who helps for the wrong reasons or who is unable to manage their own struggles which could be from some unresolved trauma or difficulties in their own past.

A friend's son played for such a college basketball coach. He was so consumed by coaching that he didn't have much of a life beyond. That's a definite warning signal because these types of coaches often mask their own inadequacies—and take out their own frustrations—on their players. Instead of affirming that each of his players had value, he began with the proposition that they were all "broken" and only he and his system could "fix" them.

While he preached discipline, he cheated on his wife constantly. For my friend's son who was recruited by the man, it did not end well; he quit after a year in the program—and I honor his courage to do so.

Misfits

Coaching can be a way to fill a human need to belong to something greater than oneself, so some people are drawn to it to fill a void. This type of coach is what Ehrman, in his book *InSide Out Coaching*, refers to as a misfit. "The misfit-coach needs his players' acceptance and obedience. He needs to feel a part of the team even more than his players do. This type of coach gravitates toward youth league sports because status and title are easily obtained there. You are instantly dubbed 'Coach,' and you are handed a group of young developing minds heeding every word you say. Parents generally fall in line, not wishing to jeopardize Junior's playing time."

I'll never forget the shock, despite logically understanding how the whole "becoming a parent process" works, when the nurse at the hospital in Amsterdam looked at my husband and me and said we could take home our first child who had been born earlier that night. "But wait, don't we need to do some training or get a license or something in order to become parents?! Where is the manual?"

Youth sports coaching is similar, with very few guardrails, clear-cut standards, or expectations. And because most youth sports coaches are dependent upon volunteers, there is usually very minimal screening or training involved. Between their own social and emotional deficiencies and their lack of knowledge about what needs the kids have or how best to present that to a group of youth, misfit coaches can extinguish a child's interest or passion for a sport before the first game, match, or meet is ever played.

Frank was one such misfit coach. He was a small Jewish man who by his own admission was not very athletic and never had participated in sports. Frank had married a tall, lanky, Black athletic former track star, Tonya. Together they had two boys who had taken after their mother's side of the gene pool. With a kind heart and the best intentions, Frank decided to coach his two boys' basketball team, who were only a year apart in age. Not understanding the rules nor how to teach the fundamentals of the game, it was a long season for most involved. Frank was in over his head in not only how to herd these eight- and nine-year-old boys, but also in trying to appease parents who knowingly invested large amounts of time and money into a season where very little growth or development was evident. He had the best intentions, but I remember the season ending with all the parents complaining and the only thing the commissioner could say was, "If you've got better skills and would like to volunteer for next season, please step forward!" Recreational leagues have very little power and usually limited resources so are stuck with whomever steps forward.

Transformational Leaders

Transformational leaders help people transform from good human beings to better human beings, from good players to great players. No one in college coaching history has had more success than Wooden, the UCLA's men's basketball coach for 27 years from 1948 to 1975. He reminds us that nice guys don't always finish last; sometimes they win 10 NCAA championships, seven in a row.

Wooden was born on a farm in Indiana. With little money and no running water, he came from a simple upbringing but with his three brothers found a love of basketball early and they played every day in the family barn.

Eventually he became a successful high school English teacher and basketball coach. Wooden got his break into the college ranks when a school with a losing record and no home gym of its own recruited him to come west, to UCLA. The first year he turned the program around with a winning season and by the second season they had won a conference championship in 1950. His first national championship in 1964 began an unprecedented run that will probably never be repeated, including an 88-game winning streak.

He was known for his clear morals and values that he not only led with but insisted his players followed as well. He was known to his players as someone who modeled the values he espoused in how he lived and ran the Bruins program.

Effective transformational leadership is defined as leadership which results in performances that exceed organizational expectations. He believed that "performance beyond expectations" was built on four things:

- Idealized influence
- Inspirational motivation

- Intellectual stimulation
- Individualized consideration

Let's look at each:

Idealized Influence

A coach who has a clear vision and sticks to a core set of values is one who is using idealized influence effectively. Wooden spent nearly 10 years developing a now widely known set of values for how he coached and lived called the Pyramid of Success.

John Wooden's Pyramid of Success

Inspirational Motivation

An inspirational motivator, Wooden, an English teacher by training, loved to quote poetry and other passages his father had shared with him. My podcast co-host, Susie, shared with me that her former husband, Bill Walton, who was one of Coach Wooden's most decorated players, used to get up early and make their four boys school lunches. Inside each lunch he'd put a handwritten note with a quote from John Wooden. She says the boys would roll their eyes when asked about them, but then not long after, Susie and Bill would overhear the boys quoting Wooden to others. Success!

Intellectual Stimulation

A lifelong learner, Wooden was said to believe there were four laws to learning. The goal is to create a correct habit that can be produced instinctively under pressure. He was fond of saying, "It's what you learn after you know it all that counts."

- Explanation
- Demonstration
- Imitation
- Repetition, repetition, repetition

Individualized Consideration

"Coach Wooden gained respect by his own personal example," Bill Walton said about his late coach. "He worked harder, longer, smarter, more dedicated, and was more loyal, while being more concerned, caring, detailed, and meticulous than anyone else I ever worked with." He was focused on helping everyone not to necessarily be *the* best, but be *their* best.

He would ask of those around him, "How close to 100 percent of our potential can we get?" He had high expectations, a clear vision, and with his deep caring, players bought into his system.

His first practice of the year, even well into their championship team years, he sat the entire team down and taught them how to put their socks and shoes on properly. He said, if you didn't pay attention to the little details, like whether your socks were bunching and rubbing and potentially causing blisters, you wouldn't be able to focus on the bigger details that matter.

In other words, the little stuff is the big stuff!

Now times have evolved and changed, and I can't think of a single youth sports coach who spends time on something like teaching kids how to put their equipment on properly, but the transformational leadership principles still hold even 55-plus years later.

And above all else, his leadership came through his love of his players and his belief in four things that were non-negotiable for him. He said players needed to learn to do four things:

- Think without confusion clearly
- Love your fellow men sincerely
- Act from honest motives purely
- Trust in God and heaven securely

In our crazy times—as I finish this book, I just learned of the brother of a former NFL player who shot and killed the opposing coach during a game—we could use more of John Wooden's transformational principles woven in our youth sports culture.

Chapter Sixteen

PUSH THROUGH OR PIVOT?

*Partnering with a coach to help find
what's best for your young athlete*

Meet Cameron, a young client of mine, a volleyball player. In our introductory meeting, she sat nervously pulling cat hair off the backyard navy sectional in her mother's Santa Monica home. Earlier, her mom, Heather, had shared her concerns about her oldest daughter, who'd played volleyball the last five years.

"She's a people pleaser. She stresses a lot. She's a bright girl who's in her head and sometimes can't get out of her own way. She's on the top 13's team, but she doesn't play much in matches. It's tough traveling all the way to places like Chicago and Las Vegas only to see her rarely step on the court. I'm wondering if she should be put on the second team, but I don't know anything about volleyball; I'm not quite sure how this whole process works. I'm a musician, not an athlete. I'd love for you to speak with her and see if you can help her find some confidence and belief in herself."

As a way to break the ice with Cameron, I asked, "If you could do *anything* with your time today, go anywhere, eat anything, do absolutely whatever you wanted to do, what would that be?"

She seemed perplexed by the question, looking at me as if I was trying to catch her telling a lie. "Uhhhh, I don't know," she whispered back. "I guess I'd go to school."

"Really? You don't want to fly to Paris and eat bon bons or go to Hawaii and inhale shaved ice?" No reaction. "Have a sleepover with your friends and have dessert for dinner?"

"I don't like to fly."

"So, you like school then?"

"I don't know. It's *school*."

I took several different approaches at the runway to get her to talk about any of her likes, interests, or passions. When I asked about volleyball, barely audible, and with the same amount of enthusiasm as one would answer if they were asked if they liked chopped liver, she uttered, "I like volleyball."

Ooookay.

Now, meet Greg Smith, a veteran high school and club volleyball coach with 35 years of experience. "One of the most common calls I get from parents is about lack of playing time. The parents are trying to decipher via translation from a 13-year-old's point of view what the cause is. Occasionally I'll speak to a highly frustrated parent about why her Greta should be playing more. 'She was on the top team over Daphne last season, I don't understand why Daphne gets more time than her this year.'

"Hearing this, I assume I'm going to meet with a supremely frustrated kid as well. Sometimes that's the case, but often the happy-go-lucky 13-year-old isn't really that bothered when I mention the phone call with her mom or dad. 'Daphne has gotten a lot better,' Greta will tell me. 'I was injured for a few months, so it makes sense that she's getting more playing time. Yes, of course, Coach, I'd love to be playing more, but I understand why I don't. Would you mind explaining that to my mom, please?'"

My point is simple: parents can be complex. Young athletes can be complex. Coaches can be complex. Let's dig deeper into that complexity so you, parents, can see more clearly what might be going on in a particular situation and how you swooping in to "fix things" rarely is the right play.

Attend any travel tournament in America and listen to what parents talk about almost incessantly: their child making a roster and their child getting playing time.

Let's start with this: parents, trust that the expert, the coach, has a plan for the team over the course of the season. Don't assume it's random as to why some kids are getting more playing time than others. Start with the belief that coaches are doing their best to get each athlete the amount of playing time in a tournament based upon how much effort, skill, and ability they have been demonstrating consistently in practice over the last several months.

I get it. There *are* exceptions to this rule, times when coaches go off the rails or just don't get it right. But it is far healthier for you and your child if you start from the assumption that the coach has good intentions. And that he or she has a plan. Because, frankly, that's usually the case.

Coaches Are Complex

Coaching youth sports today is more complicated than ever. It's not like it was in the '70s or '80s when the coach would just "roll out the ball," throw together a lineup, and let the kids play. Like it or not, society has placed a high value on winning and being the best. And yet my experience has been that most coaches try to keep things in perspective.

"It's nice to win," they'll tell me, "but my true objective is to develop all of my players because I know that is what will help them in the long run." That's transformative coaching.

I've been around youth sports for decades as a consultant, coach, and, most importantly, a mother of young athletes. Most parents have the child's best interest in mind. Yes, at times, you'll encounter a coach whose treatment of his or her athletes is reprehensible. But, for the most part, they aren't the devil with a whistle.

So, let's get in Greg Smith's head to help us see things from a coach's perspective:

> The beginning of the season is fun. Once the nerves of the tryouts are over and athletes and parents have settled into the idea of what team their kid is going to be on, for better or worse, I like to set the expectations for the season with both the parents and the athletes.
>
> When I was a young coach, I had *lots* of rules, pages of rules! My rules had rules! What I learned over time is that the more rules you have, the more work falls on you to enforce them all. When one athlete "breaks a rule," you enforce the consequence. But if a second athlete does and you don't enforce it, it gets complicated—quickly. For example, if one player is five minutes late and you have a rule that if you're late you won't play, you have to be prepared for your best player to show up late and "walk the talk." This gets tricky as the season goes on and the pressure mounts to win. Over time, I found I could chunk it down to five rules which encompass

pretty much everything without getting mired down in the minutiae.

Coach Greg's team rules:

- *You are ALWAYS representing this school and/or this club. Act accordingly, in a way that would make the school, the club, and your parent(s) proud.*
- *Bring EVERYTHING you need to practice (and tourneys).*
- *EVERYTHING you do and don't do matters. It is all noticed.*
- *Going to be absent? YOU, not a parent, should text me at least 24 hours before.*
- *Do not ask to play at tourneys. Just be ready to play. Show me at practice that you're ready for more playing time.*

The addendum for parents he offers is short and sweet:

- *Empower your child to advocate for themselves.*
- *Forty-eight-hour rule: if your child has spoken with me several times and isn't satisfied with the response, then as long as it's forty-eight hours after a game, you may reach out and ask to chat. But this should always be your last resort.*

Parents, don't assume that where there's smoke there's fire. With a wry smile, one of my kids' third-grade teachers told us on a back-to-school night: "I'd like to make an agreement with you. You don't believe half the stuff that comes out of your nine-year-old's mouth about me, and I won't believe half the stuff they tell me about you."

Just because you and your child aren't getting instant gratification, i.e., any or maximum playing time, don't assume the coach doesn't have a plan to help them—and isn't acting in your child's, and the team's, best interest.

KIDS ARE COMPLEX

Back to Cameron, the young volleyball player who didn't seem convinced she actually liked the sport she was playing.

"I don't know. It's fun, I guess. I've been doing it a long time, like since I was nine. I guess I'm not sure what else I would do if I didn't play volleyball."

"What if you couldn't play volleyball anymore," I asked her. "What would you do?"

"I don't know. My dad wants me to play volleyball."

OK, as the detective in this case, here was a key clue about what might be going on here. This could be more about a father's vision for his daughter than the daughter's desire to play the sport. In this case, the parents were divorced, and it didn't appear they communicated much because while the mother was ready to throw in the proverbial towel, the daughter was certain it wouldn't be allowed and she'd become a huge disappointment to the family.

"Have you tried other sports? Tennis? Golf? Swimming? Or do you have any other interests, like music or theater?"

"I play piano. I guess I might want to be in the school play. But I don't have time."

I was beginning to feel this girl's frustration.

"My dad wants me to try water polo. But nope! And I'm awful at tennis! Swimming is boring. It's just going back and forth. I definitely don't want to play golf because my dad would make me go on golf trips with him. No way!"

I asked her about her current team and how she felt about her role. "Well, I don't play. The only time coach subs me in is when it's obvious we're going to win. Then I get to go in for a point or two. And I don't even get to go in for the role that I've been practicing. It's usually just really embarrassing."

She was convinced that the coach thought she was the worst player on the team. She articulated multiple times that she didn't have any friends on the team.

"What would you think about playing on the second team?" I said. "Then you could get more playing time, really improve and get better."

I know several girls over the years who had been moved to the second team and despite thinking it was a demotion, ended up realizing it was a gift. The years on the twos team allowed them to be in a leadership position, grow their confidence, and most importantly, play more in matches, which resulted in getting better.

"Competence builds confidence," I like to tell young athletes and their parents.

Seeing how Cameron's confidence was in the basement was a clear sign that she wasn't going to be able to improve, largely because she didn't believe in herself. When you don't believe in yourself, you assume nobody else does either.

She said she had two friends on the second team but didn't think playing at that level was an option. "I can't go to the twos," she said. "My dad wouldn't allow it."

I mentally cringed. Her eyes welled up with tears and her bottom lip starting quivering.

"My dad says he's not paying all this money for me to be a 'twos player.'"

My heart sunk.

"My parents are divorced. I've got four siblings between the two families. There's a lot of driving already. I can't ask for anything else."

Her father, I learned, had been a multi-sport athlete growing up and seemingly valued the grit, determination, and resilience that came from having his children participate in sports as he did. Nothing wrong with that. But parents need to differentiate between their dreams and their children's desires.

Cameron said she didn't feel like she fit in with the other girls, and, as our session continued, her lack of confidence showed. "I know they think I'm weird. And I'm socially awkward. And I don't make friends easily. I just don't fit in."

Cameron, despite her wiry 5'4" frame, appeared to take less and less space on the couch the longer we chatted. With her legs tightly crossed and her arms folded over her knees, she looked completely defeated, unwilling to make much eye contact with me.

Doomed. At 13. I grieved for her.

But I can't tell you how many young athletes are like Cameron. They force a necessary question: As a parent, do we push through or pivot? Do we try to find a way to make this team, this situation, this coach work or do we encourage our child make a change? Play on a different team? Try a different sport? Or get out of sports completely?

Staying active is a critical element to happiness in life. But there is zero need to be in a competitive sport if the child has no interest in it.

Peeling Back the Onion

Cameron's coach, I should point out, was Greg. After talking with Cameron, I talked with him to better understand how the "choosing-a-roster" game happens.

Sports parents need to understand their children and the team's process. The roster-building process varies by sport and region of the country, but the club volleyball process in Southern California—and plenty of other places—goes something like this: for girls ages 14 and under, i.e., middle school and younger, clinics start in the summer and ramp up in August and September. This is a great opportunity for the girls to gets some reps playing in front of staffers who will be coaching at that level in the upcoming season. It helps both sides. Coaches get to know the girls, evaluate talent, and start assessing who might fill the potential roster spots. Players get a chance to build some confidence in a less stressful environment, i.e., a clinic, not a "tryout" while getting to know the staff.

By the time the evaluations arrive in early October, rosters aren't finalized until after tryouts. There's always room to move players to different rosters but barring anyone showing up to a tryout unannounced, the staff is quickly able to assess how its roster will look. Some coaches go so far as to offer spots to the players they know will make the team prior to the completion of the tryouts.

This gets confusing to parents because it can be a mixed message. "Oh great, my kid made the team early; they must be one of the better ones!" Sometimes that's true, other times it's the club's way of "locking up" a player. Because the club needs anywhere between 12 and 16 on a team, they prefer not to wait until tryouts end because other clubs are also making offers.

Parents often want their child to be on the top team, and if that doesn't happen, they move on to another club. I know of one situation where multiple players who were "ones" the previous year made the "twos" the next, so the entire group of families left the club and went to the competition to make the "ones" team there. Is that a good idea? In most cases, no. But it's the reality of the times.

Another factor when dividing talent up to make teams is how these prepubescent tweens will grow not only physically but emotionally and socially. It's not only tricky to predict size but there are big questions about how athletic the tween is now and how quickly she will develop over the next six to 12 months.

Adolescents all have different growth projections and timing; it can be challenging waiting for them to grow when others appear fully developed.

In addition to size and athleticism, coaches are constantly trying to evaluate work ethic, attitude (both the athlete's and the parents'), experience, dedication to getting better, coachability, and what the potential "upside" is for each athlete.

In the case of Cameron, one of the big factors Coach Greg considered in choosing her was that she had more experience than most of the other players. "We like to reward hard work and dedication." What's more challenging is knowing how much she will continue to improve. If a mostly new roster of athletes is being formed, an unknown factor to coaches is predicting what the social dynamics will be. It's nearly impossible to know how personalities will mesh or clash.

A lot of my work with teams involves helping athletes develop their sense of self-awareness. "What do I have control over? What do you I need to just let go?" Athletes will often get so focused on things outside of their control that they lose their opportunity to positively impact the team and, more importantly, develop new skills and stretch beyond their comfort zones. Because if an athlete spends every moment focused on what they perceive as not fair, she misses out on the chance to get better mentally and physically.

"What I saw last fall was a pretty skilled, experienced (for her level) player who I could see continuing to grow, develop, and contribute," said Greg. "What I couldn't have predicted was that once a couple of the other players started to gain more skills, Cameron would fall behind and then not feel like she could catch up. The reality is some of the other girls were more naturally athletic so even though they had less experience, they were able to pass her in a few short months."

In short, circumstances changed, something players and parents need to accept.

Parenting Is Complex

Parents, do yourself, your kid, and the coach a favor: you've heard this from me before, but listen to your child. Is sports her passion or your passion? If not, why is she playing? I highly encourage families to do frequent check-ins with their kids at the beginning, middle and end of each season.

"Are you enjoying the challenge?" "Why or why not?"

Meanwhile, trust that the expert, the coach, has a plan for the team over the course of the season. Don't assume it's random or some bias as to why some kids are getting more playing time than others. Start with the belief that the coach is doing her best to get each athlete the amount of playing time in a tournament based upon how much effort, skill, and ability they've been demonstrating in practice.

Being a smart player and being a great player are not one and the same. "By far, Cameron knows her 'jobs' the best out of anyone on the team," said Greg. "She is a very smart kid. She knows what's expected for each role she plays when she's on the floor and can tell me exactly what she's supposed to do. Cameron's Achilles' heel is that she struggles athletically to keep up. Even though she knows what she's supposed to do, she's not able to execute it in a game situation, which makes it challenging to play her when we're in competitive matches."

So, what questions, I asked Greg, should Cameron's family be asking her.

"Does playing make her happy?"

I wasn't convinced it did. Instead, her playing made her father happy—and she wants to please him—or, better yet *not disappoint him*. If she maintains, "Yes, I want to continue to play," Greg suggested his best course of action would be to meet with the family about what level is appropriate for the following year. He would suggest she play on a twos team where, first and foremost, she has some friends. With less competition, perhaps she'd feel as if she could start to earn more playing time.

But if she shows a curiosity about martial arts or cycling or surfing or any other individual sport where it's not as important for her to "fit in," the family should support that. Why? Because it opens up the possibility for new challenges and growth, which would help instill in Cameron things she is lacking: self-love, confidence, inner peace, and happiness. Because after all, this is childhood; it's supposed to be filled with fun!

Not everyone is cut out for team or competitive sports— and that is just fine. Help your child by parenting the one you have, not the one you *wish* you had. This is so important I'm going to say it again: *Help your child by parenting the one you have, not the one you wish you had.* Just because she doesn't have the same passion for the game that you or her siblings might have doesn't make her "damaged goods." It simply makes her like all the rest of us: struggling to find our places in the world.

Advice for parents trying to navigate if it's time to push through or pivot:

- **Check-in with your child.** Do this early and often during the season.
- **Identify support.** Encourage your child to speak to their coach directly and ask them to come away with two or three suggestions regarding what specific actions they can take (e.g., coming early, staying late, getting private coaching, working with a teammate, memorizing drills/plays, etc.).

- **Competence builds confidence.** Sometimes taking a step backward (moving to a lower-level team) can help an athlete gain footing and stability so they continue to play and learn. It is difficult to see kids play to the point of quitting out of embarrassment rather than choosing to pivot if/when the time is right.
- **Check your ego.** Is your child playing on the ones team because you want them to? Or, regardless of playing time, is your child playing because he or she *wants* to?

PART V

STRATEGY IV: DREAMING BIG

Chapter Seventeen

THE RECRUITING GAME

*Understanding what college coaches want
and what your kid needs*

WE'VE SPENT MUCH OF THE BOOK emphasizing how the youth athletic journey is not about playing sports in college, but about how the gifts of playing youth sports are the life lessons learned along the way. That said, there are kids who dream about playing their sport after high school.

In addition to having played DI volleyball myself, I've coached clients through the recruiting process as well as two of my three children, so I have some insights to share both personally and professionally. Thus, it seemed appropriate to finish with a chapter that will offer context to the ever-evolving recruiting landscape and tips on how to support your child in pursuing this path, provided that's what *they* want.

The Ever-Evolving Recruiting Process

Lesson I in the recruiting game is understanding that it's constantly changing: NCAA rules, individual schools' interest—or lack of interest—in your kid, and perhaps your kid's interest in this school or that. As a parent, you almost need your head on a swivel. For example, you need to understand the difference between "live periods" (when DI coaches can speak to an athlete) and "dead periods" (when DI coaches are not allowed to watch in person or communicate with an athlete). Not to mention having a feel for what your child really wants and an idea of how to put together a recruiting email campaign—all while making sure your athlete is keeping her academics a priority so she can qualify for these schools.

Neither of our sons, CJ and Parker, had a single offer from any level to play college basketball coming out of high school. But both were able to eventually find their dream school and land scholarships. While CJ is a third-year athlete at Boston University, Parker is in the middle of the recruiting process, so I'm living it right now, which makes it timely to share. Neither were straightforward nor easy but here is how they did it. Let's start with CJ.

I can still see the missed shot at the buzzer signaling a triple-overtime loss for CJ's high school team in a March 2019 California Southern section playoff game. After 12 years of chasing down a dream, this was the last high school basketball game for the nine seniors. On the way home, CJ wept softly in the backseat.

"I'll never play with James or Anthony again," he said. "I can't believe it's over. It wasn't supposed to end this way."

CJ's dreams of playing college basketball started at age six in his first YMCA Snuffy game. My husband, Evan, recalls a car ride home where CJ excitedly shared his dream to one day play for Duke and then in the NBA, as if it was a foregone conclusion.

"How many boys do you think get to play basketball in college?" Evan asked the first grader.

CJ casually shrugged, not having a clue. "Millions?"

In reality, 550,000 boys play high school basketball. Less than 5–6 percent get the chance to play in college. Little did that bright-eyed boy know how challenging it would one day be to make a top club team or a varsity high school team, much less get recruited by a Division I, II, or III school. And you can forget the NBA; that's a pipe dream. Less than 1.2 percent make the leap to the NBA from college.

The morning after the season-ending loss, I went into his room to wake him up for school, fully expecting the covers to fly up over his head and to hear a muffled refusal to get out of bed. Much to my shock, he looked me dead in the eye.

"Mom," he said. "I've got to get to work."

Excuse the segue into what's clearly a personal story for me, but showing, they say, impacts a reader more than telling, so indulge me as I use CJ's and his brother's experiences to explain the recruiting game.

CJ was a late bloomer. While he had some strong shooting skills early (thanks to his dad's long hours teaching him in the driveway), he hit puberty late. Freshman year, he was 5'8", 130 pounds soaking wet, not exactly varsity material. But each year of high school he grew a couple inches. By his senior year, he had started to get lanky, now 6'4", but not at all muscular.

"You're not going to like what I have to say, but I'm going to be honest with you," the director of the club told him. "You are not DI material right now. You don't pass the 'eye test' and while you have moments of great playing, you aren't consistent enough. Perhaps you can play DII, but I think you're probably more of a DIII player right now."

Before his senior year, he attended a college camp back east where a prep school coach told him that if he wanted to come to his school, Vermont Academy, CJ could do what's called a "post grad" (PG) year. This would give him time to fill out physically, work on his game and mental toughness, and play at a higher level, the New England Preparatory School Athletic Council (NEPSAC). The NEPSAC league, while still high school, is highly regarded by college coaches. The experience could raise some interest in him from DI schools. But the coach pointed out that he couldn't promise CJ anything. How far CJ went would be up to him.

CJ loved this idea. He told us he didn't want to look back on his basketball career 10 years from now and wonder if he could have played at the DI college level. If he was all-in, we were, too. But there were going to be a few hurdles to clear with no guarantee of a positive outcome.

Parents, there are no guarantees in life, so if this is something your kid wants to do—and are willing to delay the gratification of getting to college immediately—this is an option, provided, of course, that you can afford it. Some of these prep schools have scholarships, so where there's a will, there's a way.

With the help of his basketball club's director, CJ identified some of the top prep schools, spoke to the coaches to see if they had a need for his position on their team and applied to see where he might be accepted. In addition, he researched what it was going to take to make it to being a contender for a scholarship at the college DI level.

"I felt if I did all that was in my control, I would put myself in the best position to get some offers," he said, looking back. "I didn't have control over whether they offer me a position, but I did have 100 percent control over how hard I worked and what my attitude was. I knew I had to put in the time, do the mental and physical work, change my diet; this was one me."

From March 2019 until the first time he'd have the opportunity to play in front of 150 college coaches three months later, he bet on himself and got excited to attend Vermont Academy (VA). He had two high school teammates who were going on to play DI basketball, so the three of them dedicated themselves to being gym rats.

He worked with a skills trainer to improve his shot, footwork, agility, and killer mindset. And he played a ton of one-on-one against his 6'9" high school teammate, James, who could push him around and challenge him to go harder than he thought he could. Often, they would do a morning workout before school, then hit the weight room after school and get back to the gym to get more shots up after homework was done.

When CJ showed up in Milton, Massachusetts, at the end of June 2019, he was "locked and loaded." He played with his new VA teammates in front of dozens of college coaches with a quiet confidence and ease that showed he deserved to be there.

One DI college coach later said to me, "I had seen him play before and he was always a good shooter, but something has changed in the last few months. He's different. He's cheering the loudest on the bench, he's high fiving his teammates after every play. He's a leader and his smile says it all. You can tell he's just happy being out there. I want to recruit kids who love the game of basketball and get joy from playing. CJ's swagger tells me that he loves hoops. By the way, where did he get that swagger? That's something you can't teach! I know. I've been coaching for 20 years, and I don't see it often."

CJ's memory of the Massachusetts experience?

"I was prepared. In March, I wrote down 25 colleges I'd love to get recruited by. I focused on the specifics of what I loved about each school: the hoops, the location, the educational offering, the conference they played in, etc. I made the goal as specific and detailed as I could and then worked every day in that direction. By the time I showed up in front of the college coaches in June, I promised myself I would go in there so prepared, the only mindset I would be focused on would be dominating at my position and making my teammates look great. My mom and I discussed my big audacious goal—to get five to 10 Division I schools interested in me, so that by the time I arrived on VA's campus for school in September, it was indisputable that I was a DI player. I felt if I did all that was in my control, I would put myself in the best position to get some offers."

Everything clicked that first weekend in Massachusetts. Before the second weekend, we had a few days together, so CJ and I got in the car and visited every school that had showed interest in him: five East Coast schools in five days.

With each unofficial visit, we spoke about what he wanted to get out of each meeting. The goals were to see not only what the different campuses looked like, but how the staff approached him and how they responded to his questions. He also needed to see if he could imagine himself playing there and, more importantly, being a student there for four years.

Several coaches praised us for taking this effort. Said one, "That shows us how interested you are in our program and that matters a lot to us. We are looking for players who want to be here."

Lessons to remember: when you have a goal, do the little stuff. Show up. If your son has interest in that school, show them you do too by connecting with them and seeing if you can get an unofficial visit. Unofficial visits are ones that you pay for, but they are allowed to show you around the campus and answer any questions you have. Coaches love it when players are driven to reach out and take the time to show up. This can be a game-changer.

Of all the schools we visited that week, the Army West Point visit was the most memorable. Head coach Jimmy Allen ended our visit with an incredible gift. We were sitting in his office after a day of touring the incredibly historic facilities and meeting with several of the faculty and staff.

"I've watched you play several times, CJ, and clearly you're a strong basketball player. We see the potential in you to develop into an impact player in the Patriot League. But today spending time with you and your mom, I got to witness something far more important to me. I got to see the person you are, the character you have and hear what you value. I don't recruit basketball players, I recruit high-character kids. You're an impressive young man. You have energy, passion, intellect, likability, and work ethic. You have it all! So, I'd like to make you an offer to play basketball at West Point. We think you'd be a wonderful fit for us."

CJ and I were in shock. I looked over as he sat catatonic on the couch next to me. Slowly, a huge Cheshire grin crept across CJ's face. The dream he'd prayed for each night as he drifted off to sleep was finally coming true. He was being offered the chance to play DI basketball—eight weeks before he'd start attending school for his PG year.

When CJ and I got to the car, he said, "Mom, I gotta call my boys!" He put them on speaker phone and they screamed to one another like eight-year-old girls. I loved it. It was amazing to hear how excited they were for him. He's so lucky to have friends who loved him and supported his dreams.

But that was just the start. By the end of the second weekend of play, CJ had 12 DI offers. Once West Point offered, the dam broke. Others took note and after the Army offer was posted on Twitter, offers flooded in, several from schools whose coaches hadn't even watching him play in person. We were shocked! Two schools even offered for him to come in 2019, just a few weeks later. He was so flattered. He thanked them profusely but said, "I made a commitment to Coach Alex Popp at VA and I'm going to honor that."

For the next eight weeks, CJ manned the phones. He spent hours and hours talking to coaches, letting them get to know him while he learned about their programs and schools. Per the NCAA recruiting rules, he would be allowed to take five official paid visits, which are usually done once school is in session so the recruit can meet the players, sit in on a class or two, and see what the campus feels like when it's bustling with activity. What's more, he'd get a chance to go hang with the players at night, away from the coaching staff, so he could hear all about what the players loved and didn't love about the school and program directly from them.

Ultimately, CJ narrowed his list down to three schools he thought had what he was looking for in a college experience. He'd gone back to that list he'd created in March and looked at their ranking, conference, educational offering, and location.

"This is not just a four-year plan, this is a 40-year plan," he said. "I want to set myself up for success beyond basketball. I'm so grateful to have this opportunity. Maybe not getting recruited during my senior year was exactly what I needed to appreciate how unlikely it is to happen and how hard I need to work to make it a reality."

So what had we learned from this experience? As a former DI volleyball player myself, I'd been through this as an athlete. As a Peak Performance Coach, I had advised parents and their athletes, many who had the desire to play their sport in college. But going through it myself as a parent, I came away with quite a few insights.

RECRUITING PROCESS INSIGHTS

First, be clear on *who* is driving the process. If your child wants to play at the next level, it has to be their dream. As bad as you may want them to play, if it's not their choice, there's little chance it will work out in the long run. There's just too much work that goes into it, so if it's not what they truly desire, it won't make for a successful college career, nor will it help your relationship over time. If this is your child's dream and they aren't getting recruited, encourage them to be curious and ask lots of questions. This is most likely the biggest decision they will make in their life thus far. You wouldn't recommend them marrying the first person they dated without getting to know them first, right? Likewise, the better they can get to know what it is they are looking for (size of school, location, coaching style, offers of majors, weather, etc.), the easier it will be for them to "know it when they see it." It was through answering all these questions that we started to understand what CJ truly wanted and needed.

Second, encourage your kid throughout the recruiting process. Take notes in a journal after each visit and/or call. What did they like or not like about what was discussed? For example, one of the schools CJ was talking to was located in a rural area. But he is a kid who loves big, dirty, gritty cities. He had convinced himself that wouldn't matter because the program and school were so strong, but I wasn't so sure. It wasn't until he was on his official visit at that school that he started to wonder if it would be a good fit. We asked him, "Would you be happy here if you weren't playing basketball?" He said, "I don't know." We told him to listen to his gut and keep looking. In the end, he might end up deciding to go there, but if he did, at least he'd have vetted it, to make sure he was choosing it for the right reasons.

Third, determine your kid's priorities. Are academics most important? Or is the level of play the most important thing? Knowing their priorities up front helps to clarify their fit with the school and lessen the chance that they'll one day transfer. There were over 6,500 student athletes in the DI "transfer portal" last year. Lots of athletes are transferring for reasons that vary from amount of playing time to academic fit to coaching style to location and level of play.

Is playing for a winning program the top priority? While it's wonderful to walk into the league champion's locker room, will the young man or woman get to play at this school? Is playing time a top priority? How long has the coaching staff been there? Coaches at the DI level move around a lot, so don't put "fit with the coach" as your No. 1 reason for going there. Your kid could get recruited by one coach and before the season even starts, that coach has moved on. What about cost? Is getting a scholarship important to your family?

All DI schools, with the exceptions of the Ivy League schools and the armed forces (Navy, Air Force, Army, and Marines), give athletic scholarships. *Some* DIIs give scholarships. DIIIs don't, but you can sometimes get aid other ways. Time commitment for practice and games at all three levels isn't significantly different, though. So don't think just because your son or daughter is playing DII or DIII, they'll have a ton of free time; it can be as big of a commitment as DI.

Fourth is timing. They say when you meet the right person, "you just know." If the student-athletes have done their research on the schools and coaching staffs and met the teams, etc., when they find the right fit, and have spoken to enough coaches to be able to compare and contrast, they'll know. If something doesn't feel right about the program or school, your kid should trust their gut. What's missing and why? They shouldn't settle on one school just because they're tired of talking to coaches or are overwhelmed and want it to be over. They should make the decision with confidence that they've thought it through well, aren't making an emotional decision, and know this is what's best for them with the information they have.

Fifth, be opportunistic but realistic. By that I mean if you don't yet know exactly what you want—most 18-year-olds don't!—that's okay. It's important for the student-athlete to be honest throughout the process with the coaches who are recruiting them. Often, if they start to get interest from one school, they will also get interest from others in the same conference or at the same level. Keeping the coaches informed of where they are in their decision-making process is important because it builds trust.

Conversely, you should value coaches who are open and honest with you; it's an indicator of how they treat their players. Your kid should feel free to ask the coach where they see themselves on their recruiting board. If they are low on their list, that's good to know; schools will start by looking at anywhere from 50 to 100 athletes and will eventually whittle it down to a handful at each position. If there are three or four other athletes ahead of your kid and the school only has two or three scholarships to give that year that's valuable information.

It can also be helpful to know how likely the program is to "offer them." One good indicator of their interest is which coach on the staff is calling them. If it's an assistant, there is probably some interest but he may not be high on the list. If it's the head coach calling, you know you're close to the top of the list.

"This process isn't about my program at all," one successful veteran DI head coach told me. "This is about CJ finding the fit that's right for him, whether it's here or somewhere else. Of course, we'd love to have him, but we understand if we're not the best fit. And if there's anything I can do to support him, please let me know."

I had the nicest conversation with this coach once CJ had reached his final decision. CJ didn't choose his school, but he was a class act from start to finish. I admire how he handled the entire process.

There are hundreds of programs out there (DI, II, & III, National Association of Intercollegiate Athletics (NAIA), and Junior College (JUCO), so don't panic if it's not all happening at the same timing as some of their teammates. Each player has their own recruiting journey. No two will be exactly alike.

The biggest gift of the entire process is the journey within. Deep down, what does your kid want? And why?

Finally, it should be f-u-n. This whole process is supposed to be fun! Yes, it's going to be stressful, but it should also be an enjoyable learning process as well. The fun part is seeing your child's hard work pay off. Coaches are looking for players who really love playing their sport, which shows in everything they do: how hard they work, how early they show up, how interested they are in getting better, how late they are willing to stay, and how open they are to receiving and implementing feedback. (Surprise! Employers are looking for the same passion and drive.)

"I was recruiting a four-star player a few years back," University of Pennsylvania coach Steve Donahue told me. "I went to his high school practices six weeks in a row. By the fourth week, I started to notice the star player not going for every ball or working hard in every drill. But one of his teammates, a guy who wasn't as big, or talented, or athletic, touched every line, had a huge smile on his face, and worked hard in every single drill. He didn't have the natural athletic talent that the four-star kid did, but you could tell he wanted to be there. I want kids who want to work hard. Most kids don't know how to deal with adversity. This kid did. So, I stopped recruiting the four-star athlete and recruited the other kid instead."

If it's your kid's dream to play their sport at the next level and they are willing to do the work, get the feedback they need to improve. Encourage them to be honest with themselves about their abilities, understanding that there is an array of opportunities out there.

CJ finally found his at Boston University, where he's now a junior.

Son Two

Parker's journey ironically followed a fairly similar trajectory to CJ's. While some might think that it was a foregone conclusion that Parker would get a college basketball scholarship because it worked out for his older brother, there were more than a handful of headwinds that made it increasingly difficult for that to happen.

First, COVID had a big impact. It shut down everyone's development and opportunity to get recruited for 18 to 24 months. And then, when it resumed, colleges were backed up with current student-athletes who were given a "COVID year," essentially an extra year of eligibility. The downstream effect of this was that colleges didn't need recruits in the classes of 2021 or 2022 to the degree they had in the past.

Additionally, it was also challenging for schools to come watch athletes play and evaluate talent in person. I spoke to one DI coach who said, "Recruiting via film is tricky. You see a guy on tape and he looks amazing (perhaps it was edited?) and then finally see him in person to not be impressed at all. And, I have found the opposite to also be true."

And finally, the NCAA changed the transfer rule. Up to this point, if a DI athlete wanted to transfer to another DI school, he had to sit out an entire year before becoming eligible to play. The NCAA changed this rule so that each athlete could transfer once without having to sit out. So, for example, now

Max could play his sophomore year at University of San Diego and his junior year at NC State University without losing any time. Schools have really benefited from this because they can now acquire kids with one, two, or even three years of college experience, which oftentimes trumps bringing in an untested 18- or 19-year-old.

All of the above plus the emotional toll of not getting to play or get exposure had a tremendous impact on many athletes who now faced Mount Everest in trying to land a college scholarship. Pre-COVID, less than 3 percent would be able to get a scholarship; that has now dwindled to less than 1 percent.

Parker graduated in June 2022 with zero interest from any school (at any level) and zero offers. Having already witnessed his brother going through the prep school experience, plus adding COVID to the picture, Parker decided early in his senior year that doing a postgrad (PG) year would be beneficial, not only for recruiting but ultimately for more time to develop mentally, emotionally, and physically. He had blown into high school at barely 5'8' and a buck thirty-five soaking wet and graduated at 6'6" and a gangly 180 pounds. The prep year would be mostly upside. The biggest downside for the prep year is that while all your classmates are off at college doing keg stands, you are still essentially in high school. But it comes back to knowing what you (the student-athlete) really want and deciding what you're willing to sacrifice for it.

Parker chose the prep school Worcester Academy mostly for the level of basketball but also because it has strong academics and connections to lots of strong schools. One of his teammates is heading to hoop powerhouse Duke University in Fall 2023 and another to Marquette University. Being surrounded by top talent excited Parker and made him confident that he'd be able to raise his game, get some good exposure, and land a college scholarship as well. There are no guarantees in life, so we said, "You might as well go for it."

Thankfully, he didn't have to wait long. It all came quickly together for him and within a month of graduating high school, Parker had offers from Pepperdine University, Stephen F. Austin, Davidson University, University of Vermont (UVM), Boston University (BU), Colgate, and a handful of Ivy League schools.

He took his time throughout the fall at Worcester, continuing to play and take official visits. Ultimately, Parker felt like he found the right fit at Patriot League powerhouse Colgate. He was so grateful for the process and the ability to take his time and have so many offers from tremendous schools.

CHAPTER EIGHTEEN

THE TRANSFER PORTAL AND NAME IMAGE LIKENESS (NIL)

If you don't like it, you can leave, and kids making bank while in college

WHEN I STARTED WRITING THIS BOOK, pre-COVID, the total number of kids who would get to play at any college level was less than 7 percent. From 2020 to 2022, COVID only made that statistic all the more staggering because of a rule change that happened at the start of the epidemic. It's known as the NCAA transfer portal. And it's influenced the recruiting process enough that it, along with another major change, the Name, Image, Likeness (NIL) rule, deserves a separate chapter.

The purpose of the portal, which began in October 2018, is to enable athletes to change schools without having to sit out a year as they had to in the past. Before the portal was in place, if an athlete wanted to transfer, they needed to ask their school for a release. If another school offered them a roster spot in their program, the athlete could practice but couldn't compete for the year.

The effect was huge. Once the "sitting out" a year rule was eliminated, the transfer portal numbers skyrocketed. In 2020, there were 5,072 undergraduate transfers and 1,631 graduate transfers. In 2021, that number rose by a third, with 6,475 undergraduate transfers and 3,092 graduate transfers. As it now stands, you're allowed "one free" transfer but if you transfer a second time, you have to sit out a year. Still, the portal spiked the number of athletes competing to an all-time high because thousands of athletes who previously were sitting out a year are now competing, leaving that many fewer spots for kids coming out of high school.

Jonathan is an athlete who has been impacted by this rule. Originally, he was recruited to play basketball at a DI school. Before his freshman season kicked off, he saw the competition ahead of him on the team and he realized he would get limited playing time, so he approached the coach about redshirting. (Redshirting is when a student-athlete does not compete at all against outside competition, often so he or she can get stronger and develop skills without losing a year of eligibility or his or her financial aid.) Jonathan's coach OKed his request. Once the season was over, realizing that he wasn't going to get more playing time the following year because of the even more talent ahead of him, he asked to be released and entered the transfer portal. At this point he still had four years of eligibility.

Unable to get interest from any other DI schools, he transferred to a DII school. COVID hit right after he committed and he never set foot on the campus of the DII school the following year. With lack of connection to the team or school, he went back into the portal and tried to see if he could get interest from a DI program. Zero DI's came calling but a junior college

(JUCO) offered him an opportunity to play for them. He was soon attending his third school in three years. During that JUCO year, he was noticed by a DII and decided to take their offer. But his complicated, and often frustrating, journey is a reminder that the portal isn't some sort of overnight fix-all for athletes unhappy with their situation. Sadly but understandably, some athletes simply overestimate their abilities or lack the exposure to the right coach to make the leap to another program.

Nearly half (43 percent) of the athletes who went into the portal in 2021 didn't get an offer from a different school, and 6 percent either left the sport altogether.

In short, while the transfer portal may seem like it a great option—and it sometimes is—it doesn't work for everyone. And the trickle-down effect for high school athletes trying to get recruited is that highly selective process became even more selective.

Some coaches rely on it so heavily that their recruiting of high school players has been greatly reduced. One college coach told me, "Why would I go recruit an 18-year-old, who most likely isn't done growing, when I can go into the portal and find a kid who already has two or three years of college experience, is older, most likely more developed and can impact our roster immediately?"

NAME, IMAGE, LIKENESS (NIL)

In September 2019, California became the first state to pass a law allowing college athletes to be paid for use of their names, images, and likenesses (NIL). Fast-forward to June 2021, when the U.S. Supreme Court ruled unanimously that the NCAA can't limit education-related benefits to athletes.

On July 1, 2021, college athletes across the nation began signing endorsement deals. What is now being called "The

Wild West" of college athletics, billionaire donors can now legally come in and offer student-athletes cash incentives for charitable endeavors. The University of Texas gave the football team $50,000 in "annual financial aid" per player. I've spoken to coaches who bewildered by this new twist and have mentioned that the numbers are just too big for a young athlete to really metabolize.

"Giving an 18-year-old $50,000 per year is going to lead to some very dangerous outcomes," one DI basketball coach, who chose to remain anonymous, told me.

While some NIL deals are simple—say, selling team jerseys with the players' names on the back—others are more complex. USC quarterback Caleb Williams became part owner and ambassador of "Faculty," a grooming brand. University of Oregon defensive end Kayvon Thibodeaux became the first college athlete to create his own cryptocurrency, going $JREAM. The cryptocurrency fund, The JREAM Foundation, is a non-profit that aids underprivileged youth.

How far this will go is difficult to say yet, but it is safe to say we are taking a step away from amateur athletes and getting closer to the pro model for big time sports in college athletics like football and basketball. The effect on youth sports? It's too early to tell but suffice it to say that the landscape has changed dramatically in the last few decades will continue to change.

As the parent of a young athlete, you can either throw up your arms in frustration or accept that these are the cards our sports culture is dealing us. Though the days of "rec ball" are long gone, I contend that the essence of sports still abides. And with foresight, perspective, and a willingness to listen to our children instead of bully them into what *we* want, we can leverage the sports experience which can help turn them into more than great athletes, but into empowered people ready to take on whatever life has to offer.

AFTERWORD

AFTER A GAME, COACHES OFTEN TAKE a few moments—far more, it seems, if you're the mom who's already sat through four volleyball matches!—to leave their players with some final thoughts. I will leave you with only one, a point I made earlier:

- **Be a potter, not a promoter.** Making beautiful art requires multiple steps, which include having the proper tools. You also need to realize it all won't go perfectly. In fact, parenting is really messy. Embrace the muck that will eventually become art.

It takes patience, perseverance, and perhaps some prayer to raise empowered sports kids! And, let's face it, there are no guarantees in life. I know of sports parents who've done it well and their children have taken dangerous trajectories. But in most cases, if you "guide from the side" by listening to your child, humble yourself to keep learning, and get your own ego out of the way, both you and your kid will win in the end.

Some days you will want to shout from the mountaintops, "Look at my kid! She is so awesome!" Other days you'll wonder how you got to a place of such apparent discord. But if you're willing to ride out the seasons, lean into the discomfort, and embrace the sometimes "suckiness" of it, you will both come out stronger and better for it, together.

I'm grateful for your time and attention. Now, enjoy the ride!

ACKNOWLEDGMENTS

Just as it takes a village to raise a child, it takes an even bigger village to write a book. And this one is no exception. This has been a labor of love for me over the last seven-plus years. There were too many starts and stops to count, mostly due to my own self-doubt, but I am so grateful that I kept going even when the destination wasn't clear (taking a page out of my own book). The beautiful part about putting yourself out there is that we either win or we learn, and if we're lucky, we may even get to do both. I am indebted to all of those who have encouraged me to write this book, the one I wanted to read raising young athletes. I'd also like to give a shoutout to the few who told me directly not to waste my time: "No one will ever read it." Thanks for that, because that sealed the deal—this book was happening.

After wandering in the arid scrivener desert for the first three years, I found an amazing coach and partner who took everything that I threw at him and condensed it down and made each story stronger. Bob Welch, your years as a contributor on Eugene, Oregon's *Register-Guard* and as an author of more than two dozen books yourself made you the perfect writing partner to play catch with. And that is exactly what we did, all the way through COVID.

To my husband, Evan: little did I know then, but I won the marriage lottery in an Irish Pub in Budapest, Hungary, back in 1994. We clicked from the moment my beer glass hit the bar room floor that first night. Throughout many moves to different cities and countries for a variety of jobs, some ending because they'd run their course, others a bit more abruptly, we knew one thing was certain: we were going to get through it together. You are the best teammate, partner, cheerleader, and father I know. Man, I have good taste.

To my three children, CJ, Parker, and Kylie: you are woven throughout this book, because you are my world. You have been my teacher and guide and find I am, more often than you, the one needing to take a deep breath and let the moment pass, as it is never as big a deal as it feels in that moment.

To my dad and mom, Tom and Mary Ann Schimke: you laid all of this groundwork in how you raised my two sisters and me. Thank you for always believing in me and encouraging me to "go for it." You were right; it's worth taking the risk. It may not turn out perfectly, but you won't have any regrets later, either. Each time it didn't go my way, you were always there with a reassuring, "Oh, that's interesting. What are you going to do next?"

And finally, thank you to both my agent, Tim Brandhorst, and my publisher, Triumph Books, for saying "YES!" After so many attempts and rejections, I know I landed exactly where I am meant to be. To Michelle Bruton, my editor, you made the entire process so seamless. Being a rookie, I'm not sure if this is normal, but I'm so grateful for the partnership and support, and knowing that I gave my best effort on this is all that I wanted out of this writing journey.

Appendix A

HOT TOPICS

S.O.S. Distress Calls From Parents

While what I do isn't necessarily lifesaving work, I do know that feeling of panic when a parent calls with an urgent plea for help. It's as if the car (your kid) is flying off the cliff at 90 miles per hour and you need resources to help course correct. STAT!

Here are some quick-hit answers to the kind of questions that send that car out of control:

Motivation (or Lack Thereof)

Q: I played football at a Pac-12 school and my 16-year-old son has long talked of following in my footsteps. But his actions don't align to what he says he wants. Every time we ask if he's worked out today, he rolls his eyes. We've tried everything—threatening, punishing, removing video games, and we just can't get him to take action. What should we do?

A: This is your son's journey. Ask him why he wants to play at the next level and who he might know who is currently playing in college. This is a great research project. Ask him to interview the student-athlete. Come with 15–20 questions about what he needs to know to get to the next level. If the answers come from someone just a step or two ahead of him, it will help give him perspective as well as help him to hear the good, the bad, and the ugly about what it takes to play. And it will take the onus off you. This will either help him double down and work harder or decide it's time to pivot. If it's time to pivot, that's fine, but he should come to you with suggestions about how he's going to spend the time that his sport formerly took in his day.

Q: Our 17-year-old son is practically flunking out of high school (2.0 GPA) but had some DI colleges telling him they'd recruit him if he'd get his grades up. He was a good student pre-COVID, but the pandemic caused him to lose interest in school or grades. How can get him motivated again to study and raise his GPA?

A: Offer him support in planning his schoolwork and being more assertive in asking for help from teachers and peers. Encourage him to schedule workouts, and to identify, target, and contact coaches of schools he was interested in getting recruited by. That'll help give him "purpose for the pain."

Mindset

Q: Between COVID and a torn ACL, my daughter lost her passion to play softball. Physically, she's been cleared to play but she's lost most of her confidence in herself. What can I do?

A: Talk to her—or bring in a coach or sports psychologist to talk to her. Help her identify her biggest fears and put a plan in place to address them. Often times somebody who knows her history can come alongside her and remind her of the athlete she once was, which can help give her the confidence to become that athlete again—and more. Remind her that there's no way she could have become the player she did without some grit, and now is the time to dig deep for that grit. Finally, point out that every athlete has peaks and valleys; just because we're not all we want to be at the moment doesn't mean we can't find that again!

Q: My 17-year-old daughter is a gifted athlete who has had much success in basketball but is now, for the first time, experiencing hard times. She's used to being on teams that dominate their opponents but now the team is struggling. How do I help her push through what feels insurmountable to her because she's never had to face this adversity before?

A: First, point out that adversity challenges us, sharpens us, and makes us better. If you've always had things come easily to you, it can prevent you from finding that "next gear" and getting better. Second, let her know she's not alone. So many young athletes think they're the only ones who struggle. We *all* struggle. Third, challenge her to be the voice on the team that raises the level of play from all her teammates, so they can return to their winning ways.

Q: How do I help my daughter build resilience in a sport where she's relatively new? My high-school-age daughter has always had high standards for herself. As a track and field athlete, though, she's been struggling with finishing as high as she used to. Help!

A: Help instill in her a "growth mindset," i.e., being able to believe her own potential, even when she's not immediately good at something immediately, is the goal. I know, I know, teenagers aren't always big on something that doesn't involve instant gratification; they're too much like we adults! But help her to understand "short-term loss" (not winning all the time) can potentially lead to "long-term gains" (improving and winning). This skill set is transferrable to anything and everything she may become interested in throughout the course of her life.

Maybe in her thirties she'll decide she wants to be a culinary chef but has never taken a single cooking class. She will most likely draw on other situations where she hit a headwind in the past, leaned into it, and overcame adversity by persevering. Julia Childs did exactly that. No, she wasn't a runner in a former life, but she had never cooked a formal meal until she moved to France at the age of 36. She took some classes at Cordon Bleu and over the course of the next several decades became one of the most famous chefs ever, wrote 11 cookbooks, and did eight TV cooking series. She famously said, "Find something you're passionate about and keep tremendously interested in it."

Validation

Q: Our son is not a super-competitive person but loves to do his sports and activities. But he started to do Krav Maga (an Israeli martial art) and was fascinated with the idea of getting a black belt in any martial art. The problem is he sometimes gets in his own way when he isn't hitting marks that he thinks he should be hitting—and sometimes worries that others will think he isn't good enough. Her has high standards in everything. How do we help him accept the fact that it's OK that he's not super competitive and allow the curiosity to drive his passions without worrying what others are doing?

A: We weren't all made to be competitors. And we certainly aren't all "team sports" people. Some of the most driven people are those who are willing to be "in the ring" by themselves: tennis players, wrestlers, runners, surfers, etc. Help him understand that you don't always need validation in all that you do, that getting an opportunity to "go off the grid" and find beauty and peace in the world around you is something that not enough kids get to experience. "Forest bathing" is a term the Japanese have coined which is the practice of "bathing" in the atmosphere of the forest. There are a multitude of long-lasting health benefits for the mind and body just by strolling through nature. Studies have shown that your stress levels drop and your overall mood of wellbeing increases and all for the wonderful low, low price of free.

Vision

Q: My daughter has always been an amazing soccer player and competitor; she's known she's wanted to play college soccer since she started "kick-n-chase," at age six. Now, at 16—and after COVID—she has doubts. She recently said, "Is it OK that I don't know what I want? I'm no longer sure if I this goal that I've said I've wanted my entire life is still a driving force enough for me to pursue playing in college. But on the flip side, I wonder: Am I enough as I am without it? After all, it's always been my identity. And what if I'm not good enough to get recruited? I'm confused."

A: COVID threw a wrench into our kids' development. It's been challenging for kids to find a "new normal." According to the Aspen Institute Project Play, a study by the University of Wisconsin found that 65 percent of adolescent athletes reported anxiety symptoms in May 2020, with 25 percent suffering moderate or severe anxiety. Physical activity was down 50 percent during the pandemic according to Tim McGuine, the study's author.

Listening and allowing are two of the best gifts we can give our kids. Ask them what feelings they are having about their sport and why do they think that's the case. And then allow them to come up with some possible solutions: is it taking a break for a season? Cutting out the school or club team altogether so she gets a break a couple months per year? Speaking to someone who is one step removed from their journey who can help them?

And, frankly, they need to know that they are more than just an athlete; someone who relies on their athleticism as all that identifies who they are is going to learn the hard way that being a complete person is the better goal.

Facing Fears

Q: My 10-year-old daughter, a former gymnast and now a diver, is gifted, social, outgoing, athletic, and basically sticks the landing on anything she attempts. She's new to diving but already diving from higher platforms than girls twice her age. Still, she worries she won't someday earn a college scholarship. She's super strong-willed, which usually works to her advantage, but once she lands on something she doesn't want to attempt she will just say, 'I can't' and not even try. I don't think fear is driving this because she's done harder things already than the level she is attempting in the moment. So what's holding her back?

A: Ask her if she really enjoys diving or if she's participating for some other reason—perhaps only to please one or both parents. Allow her to enjoy the sport, from where she is at right now, with the talent she has. Take the pressure of getting a scholarship to play in college eight years from now off the table.

Testing Our Family Values

Q: I just want my kid to play a sport through high school so he stays out of trouble, gets to experience what it's like to be a part of a team, and gets a chance to be a part of a like-minded friend group. Back in my day, everyone who wanted to play a sport in high school could. But this is proving more and more challenging for our kids and it's stressing me out! What can I do?

A: I agree 100 percent with what you're saying. I wish I had an ideal solution, but the reality is, not all kids will get their chance in high school, unfortunately. Many schools have implemented "no cut" sports, such as football, track, and cross-country, to help alleviate some of this pressure. Of course, if your child is a wrestler, that doesn't really help. But I do suggest keeping an open mind and being opportunistic. I've heard parents of graduating seniors say, "Well, my son came in a basketball player and is leaving a lacrosse player." And that's OK. We all have to pivot at some point. Meanwhile, remind your athlete that there are benefits from being part of something great than them—a team, for example—and it isn't dependent on their being the star. I know lots of kids who had invaluable sports experiences because they changed their mindset from "I have to start and be a star" to "I need to do whatever I can to help make the team better."

Q: My kid is average size and weight but has been playing hoops for six years and loves it. But he's a late bloomer in his height and I'm afraid he's going to get cut from the JV team because there are 20 other boys who have already grown and developed. What do we do?

A: This one is so hard and feels so unfair. Coaches are always evaluating and trying to predict potential. Does this kid's skill compensate for this size right now? And will he grow enough to eventually be able to compete at the varsity level? The kids who are my heroes are the ones who get cut but love the sport so much, they willingly take on the manager role, just to stay involved in the sport! A friend of mine got cut from the sophomore basketball team and reluctantly took a position as JV manager. "It turned out to be a life-changing experience for me," he told me. "I learned to put others' needs above my own that season. And by tournament time, I honestly felt like part of the team." (At halftime of the last game, when our undefeated team was down 10, the coach shamed the squad by saying, "You act like you don't even care, like your mind is on who you're taking to the dance tomorrow night. Hey, I've got a manager over there who'd give his left testicle to be out there. Maybe we should let him play." The team was inspired and won by 22.)

If he gets cut, tell him to keep working on the things he can control: his technical skills, his attitude, and his effort. Maybe Coach loves your attitude so much he allows your son to become a practice player and that makes him happy and fulfilled.

Q: If my son gets cut from the school team as a freshman, should he still play club? Is there any hope he'll make it the following year or are we just setting him up for more heartache down the road?

A: Great question—and the answer is one only your son can know. Sit down and talk through the pros and cons of both sides. "What if you do work hard all year, play club and get better, and you grow two or three inches? Would that make a difference? What if you do all of the above and still get cut? Is it worth it to you?" I suggest having an open and honest discussion about this and letting your son take the lead. His gut will be telling him if he wants to continue or not.

Expenses

Q: My kid isn't going to play in college but I want her to stay active and involved in sports and she loves her teammates. I love hanging out with the parents; they have been my best friends for the last five years! But it's so expensive and we haven't had a family vacation in years because she always has games or practice. What should we do?

A: This is a family values discussion. Ask your spouse and your kids if they would rather have some family memories or honor the commitment to the team. Be prepared for a split decision but then make a call based upon what you value the most.

Once, we took a family vacation with the only 10 days everyone had off in the summer—just two weeks before my daughter's Junior Olympic volleyball tournament. We rolled the dice and when she came back, she had to work her way back into the rotations, but she got there. And we have some memories of a lifetime from that time of the five of us together!

A "Crazy" Coach

Q: My wife and I generally take the approach of "leaning back" and not getting involved with any of our three kids' sports coaches. I was a semi-professional athlete myself, so I know how competitive people are about their kid and playing time. That said, what do you do when you just don't agree philosophically with how the coach does their job? She's playing favorites, so only coaches four out of the 15 on the team. When asked for feedback by my daughter, the coach makes disparaging remarks to the players about their abilities. She doesn't communicate well with parents or players. She actually sabotages some of the players by telling others to either count their teammates' mistakes or not to pass one particular player the ball. It's a rat's nest of problems and we've had it. Advice?

A: This is such a tough one. There are probably reasons you chose that club or that team and when the coaching philosophy of one particular coach doesn't align with your values it can be so difficult. And, as with many things in life, it doesn't always go the way we hope or want it to. For starters, keep encouraging your kid to work hard, have a great attitude and get better on her own the best she can. I know that seems crazy to say, but it is often times the case that the work will have to come outside of the practice you are paying so much money for! And coach yourself to be supportive and empathetic, and allow your daughter to advocate for herself.

From Coach's Perspective

More Grit, Please

Q: I've got a great group of girls: polite, respectful, and bright. That being said, we are trying to move to a culture that is tougher, more intense, and improve their ability to focus and concentrate. They don't seem to want to have any discomfort. How do we help them lean into the opportunity to grow and get better? Dig deeper?

A: This is an all-too-common refrain from coaches these days. They'll say, "I used to be able to push my players. Now I'll have a line of parents waiting outside my door if their kids aren't feeling comfortable all the time." Point out that being pushed harder not only benefits the team as a whole but them personally. Emphasize the "small picture." So many kids are thinking big-picture stuff; "I've got to get a scholarship!" Instead, say to them, "What did you learn today? What did you do to get better?"

WE Before ME

Q: I've been trying to establish the theme of "make someone else better." Instead of always focusing on your own successes or failures, find something to say and get your focus on others on the team?

A: Encourage the players to do nice things for each other off the court. Tell them to do something nice for a teammate you might not even know that well. This will in turn lead to everyone feeling better about themselves, which will translate into a more giving atmosphere on the court or field as well.

Trust and Accountability of Self and Others

Q: My players have a recognition but hesitancy of accountability. They are generally too nice and don't want anything to be mis-interpreted as being "critical" or "mean." How do I get them to take more ownership of their own actions and the accountability they have to themselves and their teammates to, first and foremost, be competitors?

A: Create some team-building exercises that will build trust and grow each player's self-awareness of their inner voice. The better they get to know themselves and one another, the easier it will be for them to not only trust and support each other. When trust is high, it opens the door to being more honest with one another on and off the court.

Disregard for Team Rules

Q: We have a player who is always late. No matter what time I tell the team to be there for the game, he always shows up half an hour later. Other instances of disrespect for the team included the first road trip and several seniors were in the back of the bus vaping. How do we bet beyond that?

A: Respect. Respect. Respect. As John Wooden would say, "Loyalty will not be gained unless it is first given. It comes when those you lead see and experience that your concern for their interests and welfare goes beyond simply calculating what they can do for you."

Appendix B

RECRUITING GUIDE FOR ATHLETES

Top tips to help you through the recruiting process

Character

- Coaches are looking for so much more than just whether you can put the ball in the basket. They are looking at the high character intangibles: energy, attitude, and effort. How hard are you playing at all times? Are you cheering when you're on the bench? Do you help a teammate up when they fall down? Do you pass or are you only concerned about your game?
- If a coach texts you, text them back. It doesn't matter what level the program is, every contact from a coach is a gift. Gratitude is the most important place to start. There are 550,000 high school basketball players; coaches are looking for two or three players each year. If you aren't willing to text them back, they will move on.

- Treat every coach like he's calling from your dream school. They've earned it. And, it is a small sports community, they all speak to one another. If you're not kind or respectful, that message will get passed along. (See other notes on what questions to ask/be prepared to answer.)
- Write thank-you notes. This is next level. No one does this anymore. If a coach gets a handwritten note, he knows he's dealing with a player who's able to think about more than himself. Someone who understands how much work they put into recruiting you. This is a team player.

When Meeting a Coach in Person or over Zoom

- Look them directly in the eye, smile, and be polite. "Thanks, Coach." "Nice to meet you, Coach." "Thank you for coming to my game, Coach."
- First impressions matter! Wearing your favorite baggy sweats and ratty tee shirt is not a good idea. You are a brand. They are trying to figure out if your brand works with theirs. This is a job interview. Treat it as such and dress professionally; at a minimum, wear a polo shirt or button down and khakis. If you're going to wear a sweatshirt, make it your team's.
- When you go on a visit, wear the shoes that make you the tallest you can be! Coaching staff are always trying to figure out how tall the players really are. Don't wear flip flops!
- If you are interested in a school, visit it. Take an unofficial and let them know how much you like their university. They may not have even been aware that you like their school, but the fact that you're willing to make the effort counts for a lot! It's your chance to get to know them and for them to get to know more about you.

Advice from a Division I Volleyball Coach

"When I meet with recruits, I try to listen to what they have to say and go from there. I think the most important thing they can do is spend time thinking about *who they really are.* If you know yourself, you'll find a good fit."

Tim Doyle, head volleyball coach, College of William & Mary

Recruiting Tips

- As a potential future player in their program, you want to understand if you will be a good fit not only for their program, but for their leadership style, their offense/defense style and, of course, their academics. Other considerations: size of school, location, weather, etc.
- Bring your questions, and some paper to write notes and a pen. If you're too nervous—no problem, totally understandable—ask it if would be OK to record the conversation.
- Come with the questions that you feel are most relevant.
- Remember: you are interviewing them as much as they are interviewing you. This is only a good fit if both parties can see long-term success in the partnership.

Questions to Ask the Coach

Prior to meeting the coach, review the following questions and pick the ones that are most relevant for you.

- How would you describe your leadership style?
- Please give me a few examples of ways you like to motivate your players.
- Who is your role model/mentor in your leadership style?
- How long has your staff been with you?
- Why did you choose the people you did to support you?

- What are some of their strengths and what are some of your team's weaknesses?
- How long do you see yourself staying with the program?
- What is your ultimate goal as a coach?
- Can you give examples of how you coach and lead when things go well? Does it change when things don't go well?
- Do you believe in giving praise?
- Are you highly directive or do you feel the athlete needs to figure it out on their own?
- Do you believe in teaching, or do you feel players should know the game and you are just there to put the pieces together?
- How do you motivate your players?
- How do you build team camaraderie? What kind of team bonding activities does your team do?
- What happens when a player isn't meeting your expectations? Is there a process in place to help her get back on track?
- What happens when a player gets injured? What support system is in place to help him/her recover and get back to playing?
- Have you ever pulled a scholarship from an athlete (if appropriate) and/or has a walk-on ever earned a scholarship? Ask them to give examples.
- How often do you meet one-on-one with players?
- How often do players transfer? If you've had anyone recently transfer, can you give context as to why?
- What is your team's study hall protocol? Only freshmen or do all athletes have study hall? Do you provide tutors?
- What is your player graduation rate?
- What are you most proud of about your program?
- What are you most proud of in your life?
- What keeps you up at night about your program?
- Do you do any individual or team goal-setting? How often do you check progress against the goals? What actions do you take when an individual and/or the team doesn't hit a goal?

- When and how often do you practice? In season and out of season.
- Does practice time conflict with classes? Do athletes get priority in selecting their classes?
- What are some of your current athletes majoring in?
- Do athletes live together? Is it required or do they have a choice? How many years of guaranteed housing does an athlete receive?
- Are athletes allowed to study abroad for a quarter/semester/summer?
- Are the athletes allowed to rush a sorority or fraternity?
- What are the expectations during the summer: Stay on campus and train? Summer school? Is there a summer weightlifting/training program on campus or at home?
- What other resources does your program have in terms of nutritionist, sports medicine, weight coach, sport psychologist?
- How do you help athletes balance sport with academic life?
- Where do you see me fitting into your program? What can I work on as a player?
- When will you be making scholarship offers in my class?
- What positions do you have committed and what does the incoming class look like?
- Do you run a prospective athlete camp? (If you're speaking to them before they have shown interest in you.)

Questions to a Prospective Athlete from a College Coach

Be prepared to answer these types of questions from a coach.

- What are your athletic goals?
- What is your ideal recruiting timeline? When will you be ready to make a decision?
- Describe your on-court demeanor.

- What are you interested in studying? Why?
- What are you looking for in a college program?
- What will help you make your final decision?
- Who will help you make your decision?
- What do you know about our program? What questions do you have for me about our program?
- How competitive are you? Please give me an example.
- How do you handle losing? Tell me about the last time you lost a game/match and how you handled it.
- How do you handle winning? Tell me about your favorite win and how you handled it.
- Do you hate to lose or do you love to win?
- If three of your teammates walked in the door, how would they describe you? What would your family say? How would your high school or AAU coach describe you?
- What do you look for in teammates?
- What are you working on personally and with your team?
- Tell me about your family, your favorite holiday. What kind of activities do you like to do with your family/friends outside of sports?
- Describe your ideal day, from the moment you wake up to the time you go to bed. You can go anywhere and do anything (money is no issue).
- Who's the best coach you ever played for? Why? What made them a good fit for your personality?